Beyond Preference

BEYOND PREFERENCE

Liberal Theories of Independent Associations

FRANKLIN I. GAMWELL

The University of Chicago Press • Chicago and London

Franklin I. Gamwell is dean and associate professor of ethics and society at the Divinity School of the University of Chicago. He is coeditor with John B. Cobb, Jr., of *Existence and Actuality: Conversations with Charles Hartshorne*, also published by the University of Chicago Press.

The University of Chicago Press, Chicago 60637
The University of Chicago Press, Ltd., London

Printed in the United States of America

93 92 91 90 89 88 87 86 85 84 54321

Library of Congress Cataloging in Publication Data

Gamwell, Franklin I.
Beyond preference.

Bibliography: p.
Includes index.
1. Associations, institutions, etc. 2. Liberalism.
3. Voluntarism. I. Title.
HS35.G35 1984 366 84-8523
ISBN 0-226-28066-7

for
Christopher and Lisa

Contents

Preface

This work owes a substantial debt to the Program on Non-Profit Organizations at Yale University. Begun in the later 1970s under the leadership of Professor John G. Simon, that program was designed to fill an important intellectual want. "As compared to the well identified and closely watched worlds of government and commerce," Simon wrote with Henry Hansmann, "the independent sector has received only sparse and discontinuous attention from the scholarly community." As a consequence, they continued, Yale has launched "a major scholarly enterprise," whose purpose is "to place the non-profit sector on the academic map, along with government and business, as a worthy subject of systematic and sustained scholarly inquiry" (Simon and Hansmann, 42–43). When I became familiar with this new venture, I also became persuaded that its exploration of independent associations might be informed by social and political theories which were only implicitly and, therefore, uncritically affirmed. Accordingly, important questions in social and political philosophy would be begged. I was, moreover, convinced that dominant theories in American social science pervasively reflect a kind of political liberalism which I take to be seriously flawed, so that fundamental commitments in the Yale Program might be equally problematic.

John Simon suggested that I propose a study which would display how differing political theories imply substantially different conclusions regarding the nature and importance of independent associations. It is that proposal, so designed as to include a critical and constructive reading of liberal theories, that the present work seeks to fulfill. I am deeply grateful for the support which the Program on Non-Profit Organizations provided in 1979 and 1980 and, particularly, for the encouragement which John Simon gave to me.

In reflecting upon the intellectual journey that I have taken to arrive at the present work, I am impressed anew with the overwhelming extent to which I am indebted to a large community of predecessors and contemporaries, including many of whose contributions I am unaware. In the nature of the case, most in this community will not be specifically acknowledged. Among the more proximate influences, however, a few are especially important. My students in courses at the Divinity School of the University of Chicago and my associates in the Social Ethics Seminar have contributed, often beyond their knowing, to whatever refinement the argument can claim. Several faculty colleagues in the Divinity School have read some or all of the manuscript at some stage and been generous with their assistance, including Brian Gerrish, James M. Gustafson, Robin W. Lovin, Martin E. Marty, and particularly David Tracy. Also, my colleague in the larger University of Chicago, Alan Gewirth, graciously read an earlier draft of the chapter devoted to his thought and offered an extensive response. Although he may judge that I have failed fully to appreciate the force of his comments, he has nonetheless saved me from many further mistakes. I am especially grateful to Alan B. Anderson. Many of the central themes pursued in this essay first commanded my attention because he demonstrated their intellectual and political importance in his teaching at the Divinity School of the University of Chicago. His willing attention and assistance to my work since that time is appropriately symbolized by the fact that he suggested the title which now identifies the volume. Above all, I thank my teacher, Schubert M. Ogden. No other individual has so exemplified for me the ideal of humanistic thought and expression to which this essay inadequately aspires, nor more instructed me in the mode of philosophical inquiry which this essay inadequately represents. One is, of course, alone responsible for what one makes of one's inheritance. The mistakes are mine.

I express my appreciation to Rehova Arthur, Martha Morrow-Vojacek, and M. Makini Richey for their careful typing of the manuscript. I am grateful to *Process Studies* for permission to republish in part my essay, "Happiness and the Public World" (Spring 1978: 21–36), and to *The Journal of Religious Ethics* for permission to republish most of my essay, "Religion and the Justification of Moral Claims" (Spring 1983: 35–61).

One

Independent Associations and Liberal Theories

The nature and importance of independent associations in the United States has been a subject of interest at least since Tocqueville's justly famous celebration of "the immense assemblage of associations in that country" (Tocqueville, 114). Sometimes called "voluntary associations," "nonprofit organizations," or "the third sector," independent associations generally receive attention because they are thought to be, in their number and diversity, peculiarly American and, moreover, important to American life. For this reason, the following passage from Tocqueville is repeatedly cited.

> Americans of all ages, all conditions, and all dispositions constantly form associations. They have not only commercial and manufacturing companies, in which all take part, but associations of a thousand other kinds. . . . Wherever at the head of some new undertaking you see the government in France, or a man of rank in England, in the United States you will be sure to find an association (114).

As it happens, Tocqueville expresses in this passage his admiration for associations "formed in civil life," by which he means all voluntary activity in concert that is nonpolitical and which includes, therefore, "commercial and manufacturing companies." In contrast, interest in the independent sector generally attends to the "associations of a thousand other kinds," a class which, notwithstanding its diversity, is more limited, because it exists alongside of and in relation to the world of commerce as well as the world of government. Still, Tocqueville also remarked specifically upon the importance of independent associations in this sense, or at least some of them.

> Nothing, in my opinion, is more deserving of our attention than the intellectual and moral associations of America. The political

> and industrial associations of the country strike us forcibly; but the others elude our observation, or if we discover them, we understand them imperfectly because we have hardly ever seen anything of the kind. It must be acknowledged, however, that they are as necessary to the American people as the former, and perhaps more so (118).

The present study is also concerned with independent associations as distinguished from commercial as well as governmental ones.

In recent years, at least two conditions have set the context in which interest in this subject continues. One is the apparent discontent with the way in which both government and commerce have tended toward centralized forms and, frequently, toward concentrations of power. Visible instances of corruption have been glaring because of the magnitude of their consequences. Moreover, large numbers of citizens believe themselves to be the creatures but not the creators of these centralized institutions. In the name of such values as "pluralism," "initiative," and "participation," then, independent associations have been considered imperative for full social life. The second condition concerns the general instability of independent associations themselves. At the very time when they are advanced as alternatives to centralized social organization, many of these associations face substantial problems of support, both economically and with respect to the voluntary services upon which they often depend. It might be said that these conditions have heightened attention to independent associations. Such comparisons are difficult to verify. At the least, however, recent circumstances have insured that interest in the independent sector persists.

The present study seeks to pursue this interest because there is, in my judgment, precious little clarity regarding the subject under discussion. The relevant literature on independent associations represents, as any such literature should, a diversity of perspectives.[1] But a reader of this material is not sure that these are perspectives on the same thing, because the discussion of independent associations reveals widespread imprecision about just which associations one seeks to understand. This want of clarity may be illustrated by attention to the names, frequently used more or less synonymously, through which independent associations are identified. "Voluntary associations" is probably the most common term. As the citations from Tocqueville show, however, this term is in fact excessively inclusive, since it is applicable to many, perhaps

1. Smith and Freedman 1972 is an extended and excellent bibliographical essay regarding literature on voluntary associations. Among important subsequent publications, see Commission on Private Philanthropy and Public Needs 1975, 1977; Nielsen; and work connected with the Program on Non-profit Organizations at Yale University, a listing of which may be obtained by writing to the program.

most, industrial and manufacturing organizations. In the tradition of political thought, "voluntary associations" has frequently been used in contrast to "natural associations," and the latter class is said to be exhausted by the family and the state. Unless some further differentia are introduced, then, the former cannot with precision name "those associations of a thousand other kinds." All too often, use of the term "voluntary associations" for this purpose fails to include such specification, proceeding instead as if the differentia are either obvious or inconsequential.

On the other hand, those who do seek to distinguish independent associations characteristically define them as "voluntary, nonprofit (i.e., not-for-profit) organizations." Thus, for instance, a recent report by the Commission on Private Philanthropy and Public Needs found that "on the map of American society, one of the least charted regions is variously known as the voluntary, the private nonprofit or simply the third sector" (Commission on Private Philanthropy and Public Needs, 1975, 31). For the commission, however, ignorance relates to the terrain, not the boundaries, of the region.

> The sector as a whole is most broadly defined by what it is not. It is not government—that is, its component organizations do not command the full power and authority of government, although some may exercise powerful influence over their members and some may even perform certain functions of government. On the other hand, the third sector is not business. Its organizations do not exist to make profit and those that enjoy tax immunities are specifically prohibited from doing so, although near the boundaries of the sector many groups do serve primarily the economic interests of their members (31–32).

But this definition is inadequate, precisely because it identifies the independent sector negatively, "by what it is not." Negatives as such imply nothing in particular, so that this view fails to identify the positive character of independent associations. It is not clear, in other words, that all voluntary, nonprofit organizations (those which are both nongovernmental and noncommercial) have anything significant in common. Accordingly, this definition leaves uncertainty about independent associations as such. This vagueness is overlooked insofar as the discussion assumes that institutions have been positively identified by a negative definition, and just this assumption has all too often characterized the literature. Discussion proceeds as if the problem is not one of definition, and this prevents clarity regarding the nature and importance of independent associations.

Continuing interest in the independent sector, then, begs for some attempt to define the subject matter positively. In this pursuit, I have chosen the name "independent associations" precisely because it seems free from the misleading implications of "voluntary associations" and "voluntary, nonprofit associations" but is otherwise indeterminate. To all appearances, it names a class more exclusive than the former without assuming that all nongovernmental and noncommercial organizations are properly included. "Independent associations" is used here, in other words, to express the question at hand without begging the question. Given the indeterminate connotations of the term, it may be expected that answers to the question will simultaneously propose other names through which this class of organizations is more clearly identified. In order to seek a proper name, of course, the question must be so expressed that it implies criteria for a successful answer. I will assume, then, that independent associations are indeed neither governmental nor commercial, so that an answer is at least proposed whenever a class of associations that are neither the one nor the other has been positively identified. Thus, the inquiry will be open to the claim that there is nothing peculiarly significant about nongovernmental, noncommercial associations *as such*, i.e., that there is nothing both significant and distinctive which commonly characterizes all organizations that fall within this negative or residual category. Even that conclusion, however, would still leave the possibility that some one or more classes within this category may be positively defined. In that event, there would be one or more subject matters that may be called "independent associations," but there would not be a single subject matter coextensive with the "third sector," negatively defined. All independent associations would be nongovernmental and noncommercial, but the converse would be false.

Because the subject matter in question is part or all of the class of nongovernmental, noncommercial institutions, the understanding that is sought depends upon how the sectors of government and commerce are themselves defined. It is striking how persistently the discussion of independent associations proceeds assuming not only that all nongovernmental and noncommercial institutions have something significant in common but also that governmental and commercial institutions have been or are easily identified. Thus it is commonly assumed that government consists in the fully authoritative resolution of conflicts of interest in the society and that commerce is defined by the pursuit of profit. On this basis, it is assumed that the independent sector includes all organizations in which interests are related without such authority and which do not pursue a profit. But this widespread understanding avoids the question of whether the classes to which governmental and commercial institutions belong have been adequately understood. Only with adequate definitions of these sectors can part or all of the residual third sector receive significant identification.

For this reason, an inquiry into the nature and importance of independent associations requires explicit attention to political theory. Since coherent understandings of governmental and commercial associations are necessary conditions for the definition of independent ones, clarity about the latter requires a theory of associations generally. Only such a theory will provide the terms within which to distinguish multiple classes of associations and thereby to identify a class that is nongovernmental and noncommercial. Alternatively stated, significant distinctions among kinds of associations depend upon an understanding of significance in human associations generally. Although the term "political theory" has many meanings, it refers in one of its more widespread uses to an understanding or ordering of human associations in general, and it is this meaning that is also intended here. Moreover, I will seek to be as strict as possible in speaking of associational life *in general*, i.e., I take "theory" to mean the claims about human associations that are implied in the character of human activity as such.

This is, then, an essay in political theory, and it has two related purposes: to display the importance of political theory to the discussion of independent associations and to propose the importance of independent associations to the discussion of political theory. In the former respect, the essay seeks to illustrate how significant differences in political theory include or imply significant differences in the understanding of independent associations. In the latter respect, the essay seeks to advance the outlines for a political theory in which independent associations are, in a sense to be specified, the most important associations in the social order. Generally speaking, the movement of the essay begins with an emphasis upon the former purpose and ends with an emphasis upon the latter, although both purposes are present throughout.

The importance of political theory to the discussion of independent associations will be displayed by reviewing three significantly different political theories. As I have already suggested, the want of clarity in our discussion of these associations reflects the general absence of explicit and systematic attention to them in recent associational theory.[2] For this reason, the first of the two purposes for which this essay is designed

2. To the best of my knowledge, the recent scholar who has been most thorough and creative in attending to voluntary associations, especially in light of Western social and religious thought, is James Luther Adams. See James Luther Adams and the bibliographical references in Robertson.

cannot be achieved simply by reviewing the explicit perspectives on independent associations that recent theorists have formulated. Were that possible, this essay, at least with respect to that purpose, might not be needed. Thus, the inquiry must begin with theories that were formulated principally with other questions in mind and then seek their implications for the purpose at hand. With each of the three theories under consideration, then, I will present the more or less explicit distinctions within the associational order that it includes and subsequently attempt to formulate the implied understanding of independent associations.

The criterion by which these implied understandings may be clarified is, as I have suggested, the following: a theoretically significant class of associations that does not include governmental or commercial institutions. The matter is complicated because, as I have also noted, the significant distinctions among kinds of associations are precisely what a theory of associations provides. Accordingly, the meanings of "governmental" and "commercial" may themselves vary depending upon the theory in question. Indeed, strictly speaking, one should leave open the formal possibility that "governmental" and/or "commercial" are not, within a particular theory, appropriate identifications for any significant class of associations. Prior to a review of the theories, then, these terms cannot be given the general definitions which their inclusion in the criterion as formulated would seem to require. Notwithstanding the theory-dependent character of these terms, however, we do have ready agreement regarding contemporary American institutions which are members of the classes from which independent associations must be distinct. Thus, institutions which are widely agreed to be part of the formal system of American political rule or part of the American profit-seeking economy cannot be part of the independent sector. Accordingly, we may reformulate the criterion for an understanding of independent associations in a way that will be serviceable, namely, a theoretically significant class of associations that is distinct from whatever class or classes include commonplace American examples of governmental or commercial institutions, or their equivalents.

In saying that political theories are *significantly* different and yield *significantly* different understandings of independent associations, I mean that these theories differ in terms of moral and political importance. As this suggests, I hold that comprehensive political theory is, in the Aristotelian sense, a moral or practical science, i.e., its end is to inform political practice. This assertion takes issue with thinkers who attempt to formulate political or social theories that are logically independent of moral evaluations and, in that sense, are "value-free" (see, e.g., Easton 1953; 1965). I will, in the course of this essay, attempt to show that all theories of human associations are informed, implicitly or explicitly, by normative principles or moral commitents, so that the intent to formulate a "value-free" theory cannot be fulfilled. At present, in order to provide the context for discussing the second purpose of this essay, I simply stipulate that significant differences in political theory include or imply moral differences.

Because political theory is practical, a discussion or review of differing political theories should also be designed to inform political practice. Accordingly, the second purpose of this essay is to propose the importance of independent associations to political theory, i.e., to contribute toward a moral evaluation of independent associations as such. This purpose will be pursued through an assessment of the differing perspectives reviewed and the formulation in outline of a constructive theory that is in accord with those assessments. Of the two purposes that I have mentioned, then, it is the second which is inclusive. The three theories to be reviewed have been selected and ordered in relation to the constructive proposal to be advanced, as I will now try to explain.

Because political practice, as human action generally, is incurably particular, it is conditioned by its particular situation, and a practical inquiry must take into account or relate itself to the particular conditions in question. When, as in the present case, the discussion attends to political theory, the relevant conditions consist in the inherited political theories that are currently effective in political thought and practice. In this work, the selection of theories to be considered expresses the conviction that political liberalism in some form remains, in intellectual and political life, massively influential in America. Accordingly, this inquiry so chooses perspectives on independent associations as to permit an evaluation of differing forms of the liberal political tradition.

Given that this tradition has differing forms, the term "liberalism" has more than one meaning. In common contemporary discourse it is often used in contrast to political "conservatism," such that contemporary American politics is understood to be, for the most part, a debate between the two. In a less frequent usage "liberalism" has a broader meaning, whereby the liberal tradition dates back at least to John Locke and the contemporary American political debate joins contentious members of the same liberal family. With reference especially to American political life, several students of liberalism have distinguished between nineteenth- and twentieth-century forms (see Lowi; Wolff). Nineteenth-century liberalism advocates laissez-faire, that is, minimal authority for government and maximal independence for individuals and the associations that they voluntarily constitute. In contrast, twentieth-century liberalism compromises this independence in the name of certain understandings of equality or welfare and thereby extends the proper activities of government. The political theory that is called "conservatism" in common contemporary use is, at least in significant respects, the liberalism of an earlier day.

Of course, these two forms of liberalism must also have some common character in order to merit the same name. Students of the tradition usually argue that this identity consists in, or at least includes, the conviction that social and political orders properly serve the asserted or chosen interests of the many individuals so related. Liberalism is distinguished by its affirmation of human individuals as such and its insistence that the interests of each individual are properly defined by his or her own choice. Roberto Mangabeira Unger asserts that, for liberal psychology, "desires are arbitrary from the perspective of the understanding" and that, for liberal political theory, "value is the social face of desire" (Unger, 44, 67). Similarly, Sheldon Wolin says that, for liberalism, "what was important was not any 'objective' status of interest but what each individual believed to be his interest" (Wolin, 339; see also Hartz; Kariel). The difference between nineteenth- and twentieth-century liberalism turns upon questions of equality and the extent of governmental activity, but in either case equality has to do with, and government is properly designed to serve, individually chosen interests. So understood, the tradition may be traced to Locke (see Hartz) and the classical utilitarians (see Wolff). This reading helps to explain the historic alliance, effected in the eighteenth and nineteenth centuries and enduring until the present time, between liberal political theory and modern economics. Economics, at least in its classical and neoclassical forms, analyzes human interactions as exchanges relevant to ends determined by consumer preferences, and "preferences" is another term for interests that are asserted or chosen.

Still, this is not the only available reading of political liberalism as such. However adequate the Lockean or utilitarian form may be to most representative expressions of the tradition, some interpretations insist that it abstracts from a significant liberal alternative. J. David Greenstone, for instance, contends that American liberalism has been "bipolar," including not only an "utilitarian politics that seeks to maximize rights, interests, and preferences" but also "a politics of humanitarian reform that emphasizes individual self-development, that is, the capacity to master certain *substantive standards* of excellence of competence" (Greenstone, 6). Although Greenstone agrees that the former alternative has in fact dominated American political life since the early nineteenth century, he believes that the latter may be traced to New England Puritan thought, has been effectively advanced in reform movements of both the nineteenth and twentieth centuries, and may claim Abraham Lincoln as one of its principal political representatives. A similar distinction within liberalism was drawn fifty years earlier by John Dewey (see Dewey 1963), and, indeed, Greenstone cites Dewey as a principal philosophical representative for the "substantive standards" tradition. According to this more generous reading, liberalism is inclusively identified by its affirmation of human individuals as such, but there is contention within the tradition as to whether the good for human individuals is properly defined by preferences or by objective or substantive standards.

Informed by this more generous reading, I will distinguish between *established liberalism*, which I take to be the dominant and, therefore, "established" alternative in American political life, and *reformed liberalism*, by which I mean Greenstone's "substantive standards" alternative. In accord with the earlier discussion, I will further distinguish nineteenth- and twentieth-century forms of the first or dominant liberal alternative. The resulting threefold schema informs the three choices through which the importance of political theory for independent associations will be displayed. The thought of Milton Friedman, and specifically his work *Capitalism and Freedom*, will illustrate the nineteenth-century form of established liberalism. In addition to the widespread influence that Friedman's argument has enjoyed, this choice is recommended by the clarity with which his position is presented and by his insistence that he defends liberalism in the nineteenth-century sense. The thought of Alan Gewirth, and specifically his work *Reason and Morality*, will illustrate the twentieth-century form of established liberalism. Gewirth does not claim this rubric for his position, so that the use of his work for this purpose will have to be justified at the appropriate time. If that case can be made, Gewirth's theory offers the advantage of thoroughness and precision. Indeed, he advances one of the very strongest defenses for what I call the established liberal alternative. Finally, the thought of John Dewey will illustrate reformed liberalism. In addition to Dewey's assured place among the elite of America's politically influential philosophers, his thought well serves the purpose here because, as I have already noted, he explicitly distinguishes between the dominant liberal alternative and his own. With respect to each theory considered, I will seek to do three things: to present its more or less explicit distinctions within the associational order and the reasons for them, to formulate its more or less implicit understanding of independent associations, and to offer an assessment of the position in question. In justice to the authors in question, I should stress that the treatment of the three theories is selective in accord with the essay's purpose. Although I intend in each case that enough is said to clarify the grounds for and general character of the position, in no case does the discussion begin to approach a comprehensive reading. Also, I do not claim that these three theories are adequate to the liberal tradition in the sense that no significant difference from one or another would be found in yet further liberal proposals. Rather, I hold that the theories chosen are systematic and important representatives of the three types of liberalism that I have defined. Accordingly, the display of differing understandings of independent associations will be similarly suggestive of the range available within political liberalism.

The constructive purpose of the essay is to evaluate the putative adequacy of established liberal understandings and to propose a reformed liberal view of independent associations. In order to provide a central concept in relation to which the comparison and evaluation of these alternatives might be organized, I will now reformulate the distinction between established and reformed liberalism in terms of differing views of human self-interest or human happiness. I presume, in other words, that liberalism, inclusively defined, affirms individual happiness as such and that the major alternative forms of the tradition disagree regarding its material content. "Happiness" or "self-interest," then, is formally defined as the good for or the advantage of an individual, and the determinate meaning of this good or advantage is precisely the sense in which views of happiness differ. It follows that the formal definition does not imply that pursuit of one's own self-interest is selfish, in the sense that the interests of others are either ignored or considered in a solely instrumental manner. Whether—and, if so, to what extent—an individual's self-interest does or may include an affirmation of others' interests is one of the issues to be settled by a view of happiness. By the same token, it is not presumed by definition that the good for an individual is equivalent to the good individual, in the sense that virtue and the pursuit of happiness coincide. Although Aristotle identified happiness as action in accord with virtue, in part because he defined happiness as the chief end of action, another theory might distinguish between the "chief end" (or the supreme moral imperative to which all action is obliged) and the meaning of self-interest, such that the virtuous person is not necessarily the most happy.

In these terms, then, established liberal theories always include the view that happiness or self-interest is solely a matter of preference; that is, they never include an ethical criterion in accord with which the good for an individual is defined. Happiness, we may also say, is subjectively defined or determined, so that the "good" for an individual is, in the terminology of recent ethical philosophy, "noncognitive" or "emotive" in meaning. As a consequence, there is no meaningful distinction between putative and genuine self-interests, between what an individual takes to be or prefers to be his or her self-interest and what in truth constitutes his or her happiness. It also follows that the normative or ethical claims of established liberal theories refer solely to the proper relations between various individuals of whose self-interests those claims are logically independent. One might object that a distinction between genuine and putative self-interest is thereby included, in the sense that an assumed self-interest is not genuine if its pursuit violates the normative principles. With respect to the theories in question, however, this objection equivocates in the meaning of "self-interest." Because established liberalism presupposes independent definitions of the multiple self-interests in the community, the proscription of some given preference is not a substantive definition of self-interest but rather a moral limitation upon the given individual's pursuit of happiness. In contrast, reformed liberal theories always include some moral criterion or standard in accord with which an individual's genuine and putative self-interest may be distinguished. The politically normative principles of such theories always include or imply an objective definition of happiness.

I intend to argue that the preferential or established liberal view of happiness is untenable and to propose a reformed liberalism which, in this respect, offers a more coherent perspective on independent associations. The character of the argument circumscribes its possible achievements. Because the discussion compares alternatives within the liberal tradition, it does not approach an evaluation of the full range of options in political theory. Most especially, it leaves for another inquiry those theories which take their principal bearings within the Marxist political tradition and, more generally, theories, classically conservative as well as Marxist, for which social classes rather than individuals are the principal focus of interpretation. Moreover, the several liberal alternatives themselves are evaluated only with respect to their views of individual happiness or self-interest. There are, of course, many other issues in political theory, and they are not systematically addressed here, except by implication. Accordingly, the critical argument and constructive proposal can claim no more success than explicit attention to the issue of happiness permits.

The attempt to give reasons for a reformed liberal theory dictates the order in which the three theories will be reviewed. Friedman and Gewirth will be considered in chapters 2 and 3 as examples of established liberalism, and Friedman prior to Gewirth, because the established liberal or preferential view of happiness is most clearly affirmed in his thought. Having displayed each political theory in relation to its moral foundations, and having in each case derived the more or less implicit understanding of independent associations, I will in each case argue that the moral theory in question is internally incoherent and that this incoherence is directly related to the established liberal view of happiness. So to argue, of course, does not itself demonstrate that the preferential view of happiness is wrong; the possibility is left open that some other established liberal theory may avoid such incoherence. But I will suggest that the difficulties in Friedman and Gewirth might be expected, by showing that this view of happiness inflicts upon the two theories (and, by implication, upon all established liberalism) an apparent problem that I will call the "partialist fallacy." I use this term to name the affirmation, which I will argue is present in both Friedman and Gewirth, that some part or aspect of human activity may be morally evaluated even though the action as a whole is nonmoral or solely preferential. However, the qualifier "apparent" will be important in these early chapters, because the fallacious character of this affirmation will be suggested on grounds which are simply intuitive in character.

In chapter 4 I will pause in the review of theories to show that this apparent fallacy is indeed a philosophical inconsistency. This chapter will argue that human activity as such entails a comprehensive evaluative principle, such that an ethical criterion for self-interest is implied and the established liberal view of happiness must be false. Simultaneously, the argument will seek to set the ethical terms in accord with which a more successful theory may be advanced. Dewey's reformed liberalism will be reviewed in chapter 5. Having displayed his political theory in relation to its moral foundations and derived its implied understanding of independent associations, I will show that Dewey's proposal conforms in large measure to the terms for success which I will have previously clarified. But I will also argue that this theory is incoherent because Dewey's pragmatism is inconsistent with his ethical principle. Accordingly, the final chapter will argue that a comprehensive ethical principle must be metaphysical in character and will outline a constructive position in metaphysics in accord with which Dewey's theory of associations may be largely appropriated. The result will be a proposed political theory in which independent associations may justly be called the "first sector," because they constitute, in a sense to be specified, the most important class of associations in our public life.

Two

Nineteenth-Century Established Liberalism Milton Friedman

The inquiry into liberal perspectives on independent associations begins with the thought of Milton Friedman. His widely discussed volume *Capitalism and Freedom* (1962), supplemented by the more recent *Free to Choose* (1980), includes at least the outlines of a theory of associations.[1] This theory is presented here as an illustration of nineteenth-century, established liberalism, which was characterized in the first chapter as the affirmation of minimal authority for government, maximal independence for individuals and the associations that they voluntarily constitute, and the preferential view of self-interest or happiness. That Friedman's thought does indeed illustrate this liberal alternative can be fully clear, of course, only subsequent to an exposition of his theory. But it is worth noting at the outset that he himself calls his thought "liberalism in its original sense" and specifies that this sense is the meaning that was current "in the nineteenth century" (1962, 6, 5). The similarity between Friedman's meaning and the summary characterization I have formulated may be clarified by pursuing his claim that "freedom of the individual . . . [is] our ultimate goal in judging social arrangements" (1962, 12).

1. It might have been more accurate to call this a discussion of the thought of Milton and Rose Friedman, since *Free to Choose* was co-authored by the Friedmans, and the title page of *Capitalism and Freedom* noted the assistance of Rose D. Friedman. Still, *Capitalism and Freedom* did appear under Milton Friedman's name, and, because my discussion draws principally upon that earlier volume, I have chosen to present what follows as his theory. The discussion so focuses because *Capitalism and Freedom* is, as the later volume itself acknowledges, the more theoretical of the two. "*Free to Choose* is a less abstract and more concrete book. Readers of *Capitalism and Freedom* will find here a fuller development of the philosophy that permeates both books—here, there are more nuts and bolts, less theoretical framework" (1980, ix).

Freedom and Capitalism

In Friedman's usage, freedom as a value has to do with the "interrelations among people" (1962, 12). Its opposite is human coercion, such that freedom is the absence of coercion by other people. As one consequence, the principle of freedom "has nothing to say about what an individual does with his freedom" (1962, 12), except insofar as what one does relates him or her to others. "There are thus two sets of values that a liberal will emphasize—the values that are relevant to relations among people, which is the context in which he assigns first priority to freedom; and the values that are relevant to the individual in the exercise of his freedom, which is the realm of individual ethics and philosophy" (1962, 12).

Because freedom is their ultimate goal in judging social arrangements, liberals are inherently suspicious of state or governmental activity. Friedman's understanding of the state is traditional, namely, the state is an association that is involuntary because it is one to which all individuals in the society must belong. In other words, governmental activity in principle relates each individual to all others. For this to occur without any coercion, unanimity must reign regarding the action to be taken. But unanimous democracy "is, of course, an ideal" (1962, 24) and, in most cases, an impossible one. In practice "we must perforce accept something less," and at best "we are . . . led to accept majority rule in one form or another as an expedient" (1962, 24). Thus, governmental activity generally involves coercion of at least a minority. The liberal is suspicious of the state, because "every act of government intervention limits the area of individual freedom directly" (1962, 32).

In contrast to government, nongovernmental (or, as Friedman prefers, private) relationships can be voluntary or free from coercion. In addition to being private, however, relationships are voluntary only if they meet two other necessary conditions. First, the individuals in question must be informed; they must know what they are doing. Second, the individuals must be, as Friedman puts it, "effectively free to enter or not enter" the relationship (1962, 14). Effective freedom implies a number of circumstances, including the absence of force or deception and the assurance that voluntary contracts will be fulfilled or enforced. It also means, Friedman holds, that individuals have "nearly equivalent alternatives" (1962, 28) to the relationship in question. In a company town, the employee with little prospect of mobility does not have a truly voluntary relationship with his or her employer.

Because liberalism advocates private, voluntary relationships, Friedman holds, it implies capitalism. As generally used, of course, "capitalism" refers to specifically "economic" relationships—and, however the term "economic" may be defined, it is not thought to exhaust the category of private relationships. Thus, to move from maximizing private, voluntary relationships to the term "capitalism" may seem unnecessarily confining. It is true that Friedman frequently seems to use "capitalism" with a narrower economic meaning. Nonetheless, he also stretches the term, such that virtually all private relationships could be capitalist. In this sense, "capitalism" simply refers to private transactions that are mutually voluntary. By the same token, he stretches the term "economic" to mean relationships of exchange, and views virtually all private transactions as such relationships. Thus, to advocate private, voluntary relationships is to seek maximal capitalist ones, in the sense that the social order should be capitalist wherever possible. Since "monopoly implies the absence of alternatives and thereby inhibits freedom of exchange" (1962, 28), that is, since it compromises effective freedom, "capitalism" means "competitive capitalism." Friedman summarizes: "A working model of a society organized through voluntary exchange is a free private enterprise exchange economy—what we have been calling competitive capitalism" (1962, 13). Finally, another term for "competitive capitalism" is "the free market," so that the principle of freedom leads to the imperative "maximize free market relationships."

I have already mentioned that Friedman's liberal is suspicious of the state because it is invariably coercive in some measure. At first blush, the affirmation of mutually voluntary relationships might seem to imply even more. Since government is involuntary, one might conclude that all relationships should be private or nongovernmental, so that Friedman's theory is anarchistic. But this conclusion would assume that voluntary exchanges could be maximized in the absence of government. To the contrary, Friedman holds, maximal freedom is impossible unless the social order is governed, so that the principle of freedom implies a state. By the same token, however, governmental activity should occur only insofar as this is necessary to maximize mutually voluntary transactions. The principle of freedom provides both the justification for and the limitation upon the state: government's invariably coercive activity is warranted because, but only insofar as, it prevents the greater coercion that would occur in its absence.

There are two principal tasks for government. The logically prior purpose is to establish, enforce, and defend a "general . . . legal framework" (1962, 25) within which voluntary or free-market relationships occur. As Friedman puts it, government is to be a "rule maker and umpire" in the "game" of private transactions (1962, 25)—and this includes the maintenance of law and order, the definition of property rights, the enforcement of contracts, the prevention of monpolies, and the provision of a monetary system. Because the state must protect the "game" itself from extra-societal coercion, one of its tasks is national defense (see 1962, 23). The need for a rule maker and umpire arises "because absolute freedom is impossible" (1962, 25); the exercise of freedom by one individual can conflict with the freedom of others. It is the function of rules to define how these conflicts are to be settled, i.e., to specify the legitimate exercise of freedom. Indeed, as Friedman notes, without such rules not only effective freedom but the very notion of a "private individual" loses its "substance" (1962, 14), because there is no way to identify when an individual's freedom should be protected. "The organization of economic activity through voluntary exchange," then, "presumes that we have provided, through government" (1962, 27), a framework for nongovernmental relationships.

The second principal task for the state is to intervene in particular cases where "strictly voluntary exchange is either exceedingly costly or practically impossible" (1962, 28; see also 1980, 30–33). These are cases in which the free market does not work, in the sense that private relationships would involve more coercion than does appropriate state intervention. One such kind consists in those situations where "technical conditions make a monopoly the natural outcome of competitive market forces" (1962, 28), so that public regulation or management may be required. Some utilities are possible instances of "technical monopoly." Another class of such cases are those which involve "neighborhood effects," effects upon third parties who cannot be feasibly charged or recompensed for the benefit received or the cost incurred (1962, 30). Private exchanges, Friedman illustrates, may pollute the environment of other parties. Finally, there are cases of individuals, especially "madmen and children" (1962, 33), who must be protected because they cannot adequately know what they are doing and, therefore, are not capable of voluntary exchanges. Toward these people, some measure of governmental paternalism is necessary. In the case of children, at least, paternalism presumably involves some assurance that they will grow and be educated, so that the paternalism should be temporary.

As the state (1) establishes, enforces, and defends a framework for the free market and (2) intervenes in particular cases of "market-failure" (1980, 31), it is constrained by the principle of freedom to proceed with minimal coercion. We return, in other words, to the normative status of democratic procedures. Friedman holds that the liberal position is internally coherent because the goal of maximizing free-market relationships is most consistent with maintaining democratic forms of government. "Economic freedom," as he puts it, "is an indispensable means toward the achievement of political freedom" (1962, 8). In defense of this claim, he argues that political dissent, at least insofar as it must be organized in order to be effective, requires economic resources, and economic freedom insures that such resources are not under the control of those who occupy governmental positions and against whom the dissent is directed (1962, 16–21).

It may be helpful to summarize the preceding argument. Freedom, understood as the absence of coercion by other people, is the normative principle of human relationships. Because governmental activity is (the ideal case of unanimous democracy aside) necessarily coercive in some measure, and private relationships are not, the social order ought to maximize private, voluntary transactions. But this implies maximizing competitive capitalism or free-market relationships, in the sense that such relationships should occur wherever possible. Maximizing the free market both presumes and protects a democratic government which establishes and maintains a framework for voluntary exchanges, and the principle of freedom requires that this government intervene in particular cases where the market does not work.

Now that we have seen what follows from the principle of freedom, it will be instructive to ask why this principle constitutes "our ultimate goal in judging social arrangements." Just because the principle is ultimate, it might be said that this question cannot properly be asked; freedom simply is Friedman's fundamental normative affirmation. In reply, one might note that fundamental normative affirmations themselves require justification. Nonetheless, the question of justification is not the matter to which I here refer. Rather, one might ask why freedom is our ultimate goal because, in accord with this principle, good human relationships have been identified negatively; they are defined as the absence of coercion, and one wonders whether there is anything positive involved. To be sure, the absence of coercion itself includes some positive elements; for instance, an individual participates in a democratic state which defines the rules of the game and he or she has sufficient information to be genuinely voluntary. Still, the absence of coercion is not prescribed in order for these elements to be present; rather, these are conditions requisite for the absence, such that the question persists—what, in positive terms, is freedom for?

Although Friedman does not explicitly raise this question, his answer to it is readily apparent in the following statement: "The possibility of co-ordination through voluntary cooperation rests on the elementary—

yet frequently denied—proposition that both parties to an economic transaction benefit from it, provided the transaction is bilaterally voluntary" (1962, 13). In such transactions, he explains, each independent household (or individual) "uses the resources it controls to produce goods and services that it then exchanges for goods and services produced by other households, on terms mutually acceptable to the two parties to the bargain." Each "is thereby enabled to satisfy its wants indirectly." Households or individuals are led to cooperate in this way because of "the increased product made possible by division of labor and specialization of function" (1962, 13); that is, more wants are satisfied. In the text, the argument is advanced explicitly to show the *possibility* of voluntary cooperation; implicitly, however, it also asserts why voluntary exchange is *desirable*. Human relationships should be free because thereby the want-satisfaction of all who are involved will be increased. Humans are understood, in other words, as creatures who seek to satisfy wants and who have an equal right, or who should be equally free, to do so.

It follows from what has been said that there is no moral criterion in accord with which wants may be evaluated. Because freedom is the sole normative principle, wants are solely matters of preference. Thus, Friedman's liberalism affirms the right of each individual "to make the most of his capacities and opportunities according to his own lights, *subject only* to the provision that he not interfere with the freedom of other individuals to do the same" (1962, 195, emphasis added). Accordingly, there is no normative distinction between genuine and putative wants, between that which an individual ought to want and that which he or she does want. Indeed, were there such a distinction, the fact that exchange is voluntary would not necessarily mean that the benefit to both parties is increased. For one or both parties might have been pursuing wants that he or she should not have been, wants the satisfaction of which actually lessens genuine benefit.[2]

Friedman's affirmation of equality should be understood in this light. Equality of opportunity, but not equality of outcome, is implied by the principle of freedom, and the former refers to each person's right to pursue his or her own benefit or to satisfy preferential wants (1962, 195; see also 1980, 128–49). Coercive relationships, then, do or may violate this

2. This reading is confirmed when, in *Free to Choose*, the justification for voluntary exchange is repeated with a telling addition: "If an exchange between two parties is voluntary, it will not take place unless both *believe* they will benefit from it" (1980, 13, emphasis added). That a voluntary exchange is justified because individuals so believe implies the absence of a distinction between what people think they want and what they ought to want.

equality, either because one person's benefit is forcibly sacrificed for the sake of another (exploitation) or because one person's benefit is forcibly defined by another (paternalism), and only the individual can determine his or her own preferences. Because voluntary cooperation necessarily increases the want-satisfaction of each, Friedman endorses the traditional claim for a market economy, namely, that it enables "resources" to be "used most effectively" or "efficiently" (1962, 166, 67). When individuals are in the situation of competitive capitalism, Friedman argues, they enter exchanges because they are mutually beneficial. Thus, each will find the exchange through which he or she receives "the whole of what he adds to the product" (1962, 166) and will not find an exchange in which he or she gets more. Hence, each has the incentive so to engage his or her capacities and specialize his or her production that the increased benefit to all is maximized, and resources are so allocated as to be most effective in adding to the want-satisfaction of each. "Adam Smith's flash of genius was his recognition that [the free market] . . . could coordinate the activity of millions of people, each seeking his own interest, in such a way as to make everyone better off" (1980, 13). The discussion returns, in other words, to the imperative to maximize free-market relationships.

Nonprofit Associations

We are now in a position to focus upon the distinctions within Friedman's theory of associations and, especially, to consider the place of independent associations. We have already examined at some length the theoretical importance of a distinction between governmental and nongovernmental organizations. Since government, in contrast to private activity, is invariably coercive in some measure, there is an inherent limitation upon it, again in contrast to private life. Indeed, the proper role of government is defined in relation to private transactions; government should act insofar as this is required for maximizing private transactions that are voluntary. It is this relationship that Friedman is most concerned to clarify and to develop with respect to various contemporary social problems, because he believes that twentieth-century American politics has compromised the proper liberal order by extending governmental activity far beyond its warrant. Our interest here, however, concerns the possibility of a distinction within the class of nongovernmental or private transactions, such that a significant class of independent associations might be identified. Accordingly, the inquiry here will have to seek the implications of Friedman's theory. In chapter 1, I proposed that a definition of independent associations has been achieved when a significant class that does not include commonplace examples of American governmental or commercial institutions, or their equivalents, has been identified. We may now ask whether the implications of Friedman's theory include such a class.

We have seen that mutually voluntary, private transactions are those of competitive capitalism or the free market, so that maximizing the former implies maximizing the latter. Because free-market relationships include those within or between associations that we commonly call commercial in character, there is warrant for defining commercial organizations as capitalist ones. The commercial sector, then, is the competitive, profit-seeking sector of the society. The notion of profit-seeking, so central to discussion of capitalism, has not been mentioned heretofore. But only the word has been missing. The claim that each individual enters voluntary exchanges in order to maximize his or her want-satisfaction *is* the notion of each seeking his or her maximal return or profit. Of course, this is not the more narrow meaning of "profit," according to which the term designates the return upon capital invested in private enterprise—unless the terms "investment" and "enterprise" are stretched to mean any use of resources (human as well as material) and any production or contribution to production. Nor is the broad use of "profit-seeking" restricted to transactions in which money is a medium of exchange. Since the use of money may be an arbitrary matter, its presence cannot identify a theoretical distinction. On the contrary, the significant theoretical claim concerns the kind of relationships in question, whatever may in fact be employed to facilitate them. "Profit" is used here to mean the return for any contribution to production, where "return" and "production" are measured in terms of the capacity to satisfy wants. "Profit-seekers" are individuals who enter transactions seeking to maximize their own capacity to satisfy their own wants, i.e., to maximize their own benefit. Given this use of the term, Friedman's imperative to maximize free-market relationships is the imperative to maximize that sector which is profit-seeking under competitive conditions, the commercial sector.

It may seem that this understanding of profit-seeking is so broad as to be coextensive with nongovernmental or private relationships as such. *Nonprofit* relationships or institutions, those that are nongovernmental *and* noncommercial, seem to be impossible by definition, so that Friedman's theory cannot imply any understanding of independent associations. But this conclusion does not follow. Since profit-seeking is the attempt to maximize one's own benefit, there is an alternative kind of private relationship, a transaction in which one party agrees to sacrifice equality, either because one person's benefit is forcibly sacrificed for the sake of another (exploitation) or because one person's benefit is forcibly defined by another (paternalism), and only the individual can determine his or her own preferences. Because voluntary cooperation necessarily increases the want-satisfaction of each, Friedman endorses the traditional claim for a market economy, namely, that it enables "resources" to be "used most effectively" or "efficiently" (1962, 166, 67). When individuals are in the situation of competitive capitalism, Friedman argues, they enter exchanges because they are mutually beneficial. Thus, each will find the exchange through which he or she receives "the whole of what he adds to the product" (1962, 166) and will not find an exchange in which he or she gets more. Hence, each has the incentive so to engage his or her capacities and specialize his or her production that the increased benefit to all is maximized, and resources are so allocated as to be most effective in adding to the want-satisfaction of each. "Adam Smith's flash of genius was his recognition that [the free market] . . . could coordinate the activity of millions of people, each seeking his own interest, in such a way as to make everyone better off" (1980, 13). The discussion returns, in other words, to the imperative to maximize free-market relationships.

Nonprofit Associations

We are now in a position to focus upon the distinctions within Friedman's theory of associations and, especially, to consider the place of independent associations. We have already examined at some length the theoretical importance of a distinction between governmental and nongovernmental organizations. Since government, in contrast to private activity, is invariably coercive in some measure, there is an inherent limitation upon it, again in contrast to private life. Indeed, the proper role of government is defined in relation to private transactions; government should act insofar as this is required for maximizing private transactions that are voluntary. It is this relationship that Friedman is most concerned to clarify and to develop with respect to various contemporary social problems, because he believes that twentieth-century American politics has compromised the proper liberal order by extending governmental activity far beyond its warrant. Our interest here, however, concerns the possibility of a distinction within the class of nongovernmental or private transactions, such that a significant class of independent associations might be identified. Accordingly, the inquiry here will have to seek the implications of Friedman's theory. In chapter 1, I pro-

order to increase benefit to
fined in terms of such sacri-
harity. Friedman clearly ap-
ll regard private charity di-
ample of the proper use of
ge that capitalism promotes
less laissez-faire American
n "explosion of charitable
nsequence of which he ob-
s that charity should be vol-
of freedom. Indeed, where
t is not involved), it is not

l definition of profit makes
onprofit activity untenable.
oes indeed get something in
n benefited. The charitable
ofar as satisfying this want
any other possible activity.
, the quest for this satisfac-
ossible activity. This objec-
iedman's formulations. In
t someone distressed by the
on" (1962, 191). Similarly,
e concept of self-interest,"
that interests" the individ-
e the frontiers of his disci-
viduals to the true faith, the
e needy—all are pursuing

way, and thereby erasing
nonprofit activity, recom-
one thing, the term "char-
ger say that giving to help
self-interest. Thus, Fried-
e broad meaning of self-
kindness and self-interest
make "charity" a want like
ual can produce and benefit
hungry but chooses to do
hooses to give him bread.
an exchange takes place in

which Smith, by receiving the bread, has given want-satisfaction to Jones, or has produced something by doing nothing. Friedman clearly does not hold that the recipients of private charity are thereby contributing to the "total product," such that they could be said to "earn what they receive." On the contrary, producing is a matter of human effort (see 1962, 166). Indeed, only by restricting the meaning of production so that it serves noncharitable self-interests can Friedman say that a system of voluntary exchanges uses resources most effectively (1962, 166). For, by definition, charity "wants" nothing other than the satisfaction of someone else's noncharitable wants, and more wants could be satisfied if the charitable person also had some of his or her noncharitable wants served in return. The system which uses resources most effectively is not one which maximizes voluntary exchanges, where charity is included as an exchange, but one which maximizes voluntary exchanges that are mutually beneficial to noncharitable wants.

If we wish to speak of "wanting" another's benefit, I conclude that this want is of a different order than the noncharitable wants toward whose satisfaction charity is directed. Indeed, logically speaking, this must be the case, since charity presupposes noncharitable wants; there is nothing for a charitable person to "want" unless some other person has wants of another order. But it is simply clearer to say that an individual's wants or self-interests are, by definition, noncharitable, and that charity seeks the benefit of another without return. This difference gives substance to the concept of nonprofit activity; because profit-seeking is an attempt to maximize one's own benefit, nonprofit activity sacrifices this benefit for the sake of another. Voluntary, profit-seeking relationships, we may say, are mutually beneficial, while charitable ones are unilaterally so.

Given this understanding of charity as nonprofit activity, we may now ask whether charitable associations should be found within the social order, so that they may be called a significant class of associations. The question may seem superfluous, since Friedman so obviously approves of charity. But the matter is more complicated. When he writes that charity is "a proper use of freedom," Friedman does not tell us whether "proper" means "morally permissible" or, at least in some respects, "morally required." Only the latter permits one to say that charitable associations *should* be found within the social order. Nor do Friedman's explicit discussions of poverty resolve the issue, because they assume that the reader agrees with his willingness to provide some form of assistance to the less fortunate (see 1962, 190–95). It might be argued that Friedman thereby betrays a belief that charity is no more than morally permissible, just because he cannot proceed with the discussion unless he presumes charitable interest. This argument could appeal to Friedman's insistence that freedom is the "ultimate goal" of human relationships, such that one's freedom can only be morally limited by the freedom of another. Since the failure to be charitable is not coercion, charitable activity cannot be morally required. This interpretation seems confirmed when Friedman discusses the possibility of governmental assistance to the poor and advances his well-known proposal for a "negative income tax," through which a "floor under the standard of life of every person in the community" should be set (1962, 191; see also 190–95 and 1980, 119–24). This discussion also takes for granted that most citizens are concerned about the alleviation of poverty, and the fact that this concern is no more than morally permissible seems especially apparent when Friedman comments upon the level of support: "I see no way of deciding 'how much' except in terms of the amount of taxes we—by which I mean the great bulk of us—are willing to impose on ourselves for this purpose" (1962, 191). If this line of thought accurately follows the implications of Friedman's theory, one must conclude that charitable institutions do not constitute a morally significant class. The difference between morally permissible choices is not morally significant.

But it is not clear that this reading is correct. Evidence to the contrary is found in Friedman's insistence that government has a responsibility to protect madmen and children. Private transactions, it will be recalled, must fulfill two conditions in order to be mutually voluntary—the participants must be informed and effectively free. Because madmen and children are not sufficiently informed, they cannot engage in voluntary exchange. The poor may also be understood as people to whom voluntary exchange is denied, because physical handicaps or the absence of property and employment opportunity prevent them from being effectively free. If the principle of freedom precludes moral responsibility for the poor, the same must be true of madmen and children. But Friedman clearly affirms responsibility for the latter. This affirmation might be reconciled with the principle of freedom if we recall that freedom is the "ultimate goal" of human relationships because humans seek want-satisfaction. Since those who cannot engage in voluntary exchange nonetheless have wants to be satisfied, there is a moral responsibilty to assist or protect them. The dictum that freedom is limited only by the freedom of others, then, is applicable wherever voluntary exchange is possible; elsewhere the equal right to want-satisfaction is morally controlling.

I take this to be the interpretation that is most consistent with Friedman's intentions and conclude, therefore, that he affirms a moral responsibility to help the poor. This does not show that there is a moral responsibility to be charitable, since charity is a private rather than governmental activity. Indeed, given the similarity between the poor, on the one hand, and madmen and children, on the other, one might argue that assistance to the less fortunate should be executed by the state. Friedman's proposal for a negative income tax moves in this direction. Still, he clearly prefers private charity wherever feasible, and he bemoans the fact that "one of the major costs of the extension of government welfare activities has been the corresponding decline in private charitable activities" (1962, 190–91). The principal reasons for this seem to be Friedman's empirical judgments that government programs, once begun, are rarely terminated and that the increase in government anywhere, however appropriate, tends to support increase in government generally. In any event, there is no reason why the government *must* be the agent of care for the poor. There is also no reason why the protection of madmen and children must be executed by the state. If we cannot say that private associations *should* be formed for such purposes, it is also true that organizations designed to help the nonvoluntary, or those who cannot engage in voluntary exchange, constitute a morally significant class, and that because assistance to these people is morally required.

In itself, of course, this conclusion does not mean that all nongovernmental, noncommercial institutions are morally significant, for it may still be morally permissible to be charitable toward people who are capable of voluntary exchange. Thus, the nonprofit sector may be a larger class than the morally significant class of nonprofit associations. Friedman himself seems to confirm this interpretation when he speaks approvingly not only of organizations to help the needy but also of nonprofit colleges and universities, art museums, opera houses, and symphony orchestras (1980, 36–37). One might note that the principal point of these commendations is to show that "there is no inconsistency between a free market system and the pursuit of broad social and cultural goals" (1980, 140), so that Friedman's comments do not necessarily represent a theoretical claim regarding the kinds of organizations that should or should not be profit-seeking. In any event, given the absence of theoretical attention to nonprofit organizations, the pertinent issue concerns the implications of Friedman's theory.

In relation to that issue, it must be remembered again that humans are understood as creatures who seek to satisfy wants, and that voluntary exchange is affirmed because thereby the want-satisfaction of all parties is increased. This, we are told, was Adam Smith's "flash of genius." Friedman seeks to maximize the free market (competitive, profit-seeking relationships), because this assures the most "effective" use of resources. But, in this light, one should not be charitable to those who are capable of voluntary exchange. For charity, by definition, is unilaterally rather than mutually beneficial, and, where the recipient might have given something in exchange, charity will compromise the effective use of resources and thereby decrease the satisfaction of wants. If Jones is willing to be charitable to Smith regardless of Smith's capacities, then Smith will "enter into relationships on the basis of what he can receive rather than what he can produce" (1962, 166). The want-satisfaction would be greater if Smith not only receives bread but also produces shoes in exchange, but this increase is prevented by Jones's misplaced charity. The imperative to maximize free-market or voluntary exchanges may be violated just as surely by inappropriate charity as by inappropriate governmental activity, and charity, as government, is properly limited to situations in which the free market does not work. One may say that the logic of Friedman's theory limits charity to help for the nonvoluntary, even if his explicit statements do not always conform to this conclusion.

The theory that charitable institutions are properly addressed to the nonvoluntary has considerable import for the American social order. According to this theory, the nonprofit sector as we know it in America has expanded far beyond its appropriate scope. Indeed, one might say that Friedman's commitments call for a critique of charitable violations of the free market that would parallel his detailed exposure of improper governmental activity. It follows from what has been said, for instance, that most cultural institutions (museums, theaters, symphonies and so on) should not be organized on a nonprofit basis, because such institutions, with rare exceptions, are not principally addressed to the nonvoluntary. Even less is there justification for the National Endowment for the Arts, which not only supports cultural institutions through unilaterally beneficial relationships but also coerces individual "giving" through the tax system (see 1960, 68). The nonvoluntary aside, in other words, there should be in the social order only the extent and variety of cultural institutions that people are willing to "pay for" in the competitive, profit-seeking market. A similar argument applies to institutions of higher education and to government support for them. Some minimal level of learning (let us say, through secondary school, as we presently know it) is required in order that children may become adults capable of voluntary exchange. Those without this level of education are, therefore, included among the nonvoluntary, as Friedman has recognized in his proposal for a system of governmentally provided educational "vouchers" (see 1962, 85–98; 1980, 152–75). Also, some forms of higher education might be governmentally supported in the name of national defense. Beyond the minimum, however, and aside from considerations of national security, educational institutions should be profit-seeking. Nonprofit, health-delivery institutions are sometimes designed principally to serve the medical needs of the "less fortunate." But where this is not the case, they too will be more properly organized within the commercial system of voluntary exchange. Finally, even religious associations seem properly to fall in large measure within the profit-seeking sector. Some religious communities are explicitly committed to help for the nonvoluntary, but religious purposes include many other activities in addition to such charity. In sum, if Friedman's theory permits a significant class of charitable institutions, the imperative to maximize free-market relationships also implies a substantial curtailment of the "third sector" as it has been traditionally understood.

Having now seen how the moral limits upon charity restrict the nonprofit sector, we must also note how that sector may be expanded by the inclusion of another class of organizations. I refer to those nongovernmental associations that are designed to facilitate participation in the procedures of democratic government, which Friedman sometimes calls "public service" organizations (see 1980, 36). Because democratic government is morally required, associations which facilitate democratic participation are morally significant. We may recall Friedman's claim that a capitalist economy is a means to democratic government because it makes available nongovernmental resources for organized dissent, without which the dangers of coercion by those in power are greatly increased. Although Friedman clearly approves of such organizations, it might be debated whether these associations should properly be called "nonprofit." Friedman, it might be argued, distinguishes sharply between political and private activity, such that private activity is the "game" of pursuing wants, and politics both constitutes a context within which this game goes on and insures that it proceeds with minimal coercion. Democratic participation, then, is properly understood as something like a duty, the exercise of which precedes or is in addition to relationships concerned with wants or benefits. Since profit-seeking activity is one kind of activity *within* the game, nonprofit activity should be understood in the same way. Nonprofit organizations can only be charitable ones. On the other hand, it might be said that "nonprofit" means simply "nongovernmental" and "not profit-seeking," so that nongovernmental political organizations qualify. I see no way to settle this debate within the terms that Friedman has presented, and I suspect that it might lead to some conceptual puzzles were it adequately pursued. In order to move the discussion along, and in keeping with the usual practice of including at least many public service associations in the nonprofit sector, I will simply assert that they as well as charitable institutions make up the class of nonprofit organizations.

But the sharp distinction between political and private activity implies a limit to the extent of nongovernmental, political organizations in the social order. We have just seen that politics is not properly involved with pursuing wants. But the satisfaction of wants is what humans seek. Consequently, Friedman's view implies that politics is a kind of instrumental activity, requisite to, but not itself a part of, the primary human activity. Politics, as an old saying has it, is a burden—a duty that should be performed in order to set proper conditions for the pursuit of happiness but contributing nothing to happiness itself.[3] In a liberal society nongovernmental political associations will be found only to the extent that without them the state fails to fulfill its proper, instrumental role. In short, these associations, like charitable institutions and the state itself, are limited by the imperative to maximize free-market relationships.

Friedman's theory of associations may now be summarized schematically as in Figure 1.

It is clear, then, that Friedman's theory does identify a morally significant class of nongovernmental, noncommercial—and, therefore, independent—associations. It is worth noting that these theoretical distinctions coincide with the common practice of dividing the social order into governmental, profit-seeking, and nonprofit sectors, so that Friedman provides a systematic rationale for equating independent associations with the nongovernmental, nonprofit class. We have seen, of

3. In a more recent work, Friedman suggests that a change has occurred in his thought about government, perhaps raising a question about whether the distinction which I have drawn between political and private activity remains appropriate. "This book is influenced by a fresh approach to political science. . . . *Free to Choose* treats the political system symmetrically with the economic system. Both are regarded as markets in which the outcome is determined by the interaction among persons pursuing their own self-interests (broadly interpreted) rather than the social goals the participants find it advantageous to enunciate. That is implicit throughout the book and explicit in the final chapter" (1980, ix–x). Friedman's meaning here is not easy to fathom. To be sure, politics is an interaction among persons pursuing their self-interests, *if* this term is *broadly* construed. So interpreted, self-interests may include interests or opinions about the general context in which the game of pursuing wants takes place. But just as charitable "wants" are of a different order than the wants whose satisfaction constitutes benefit, so interests in the general context are of a different order than the wants pursued within that context. Precisely this distinction is implied when Friedman says that political agents pursue self-interests, broadly interpreted, rather than the social goals the participants find it advantageous to enunciate. In any event, I find nothing in the book, either implicit or explicit, that constitutes an attempt to erase the distinction between political and private relationships. Indeed, were interests pursued in politics of the same order as those pursued in the private free market, the result would be profound incoherence. For there is no reason why the results of "voluntary exchanges" regarding political matters should lead to the competitively capitalist social order that Friedman prescribes. All would depend upon the "wants" with which individuals entered the political interaction.

FIGURE 1
ASSOCIATIONS

<table>
<tr><td rowspan="3">Governmental</td><td colspan="3">Nongovernmental</td></tr>
<tr><td rowspan="2">Profit-seeking or commercial</td><td colspan="2">Nonprofit or independent</td></tr>
<tr><td>Charitable</td><td>Public service</td></tr>
</table>

course, that the theory in fact specifies *two* classes of independent associations, political and charitable, which are both morally significant. But it is also true that "nonprofit" is a significant characteristic of both of these, and that these two classes exhaust the morally permissible nonprofit sector. At least in this sense, there is justice in speaking summarily of the traditional threefold schema. Finally, it is worth emphasizing that Friedman's theory justifies this trilogy because it prescribes maximal free-market relationships. Since the free market is necessarily private, this imperative makes the distinction between governmental and nongovernmental important. Since the free market is necessarily profit-seeking, this imperative makes the distinction between profit and nonprofit important. The imperative to maximize the free market rests, in turn, upon the principle of freedom and the controlling affirmation of want-satisfaction. But the centrality of the free market which validates the equation of "independent institutions" with "nonprofit organizations" also limits the subject matter. The extent of both charitable and nongovernmental, political associations, we have seen, is constrained by the priority of the profit sector.

Critical Discussion

It should be clear from the preceding discussion that Friedman's theory of associations serves well as an illustration of nineteenth-century established liberalism. He does indeed insist upon minimal government and maximal independence for individuals and the associations which they voluntarily constitute. He is also committed to the preferential view of happiness, in accord with which established liberalism is distinguished from reformed liberalism. Just this view is asserted in his claim that freedom is the sole moral principle and that people should be free because humans seek to satisfy wants. Accordingly, there is no moral criterion by virtue of which the good for an individual is defined. On the contrary, normative claims refer solely to the proper relationships between individuals of whose self-interests those claims are logically independent.

In order to assess this perspective on human associations, I will summarize Friedman's theory in the following three assertions.

(1) Humans seek satisfaction of wants that are solely preferential.
(2) Each individual should be free, that is, has an equal right, to satisfy his or her wants.
(3) Free-market relationships should be maximized.

Let us begin by assuming that the first two statements are true. Are there problems, then, in moving to the third? In making this move, Friedman has given specificity to the sense in which individuals should be free; the third statement, that is, implies that each has an equal right to satisfy his or her wants *given the market distribution of benefits*. For the free market not only satisfies the wants of participants, it also distributes the benefits through which wants can be satisfied. In short, Friedman assumes in moving to the third statement that the free-market distribution is good or moral.

Given (1) above, it may well be true that "both parties to an economic transaction benefit from it, provided the transaction is bilaterally voluntary" (1962, 13). It may also be true that all parties in a system of competitive capitalism increase their benefits through all exchanges in which they participate. But it does not follow that this system of exchanges is best. Simultaneously with the increase in benefits for all, the system also distributes those benefits, and capitalism in Friedman's sense is best only if the free-market distribution is also best. In Friedman's theory, "best" can only mean "most in accord with the principle of freedom," since freedom is the sole norm for social relationships. The move to (3), then, requires the prior claim that the free-market distribution of benefits is most in accord with freedom, or that the transactions in a capitalist system are truly voluntary.

The problem cannot be evaded by saying that the distribution of benefits depends upon the prior resources with which individuals enter relationships, and that the prior distribution of resources is of no ethical concern when the normative principle prescribes solely the proper character of those relationships. For the resources with which individuals enter the market are in part the consequence of some previous "round" of market transactions. The evasion will be no more successful if the "rounds" could be pushed back to some "initial" distribution of resources. For the distribution of benefits remains a consequence of market transactions, and Friedman must show why the principle for human relationships implies an affirmation of the initial distribution of resources. Why does the equal right to pursue solely preferential wants imply the market distribution of benefits; or, to rephrase the question, why is this equal right defined with reference to the market distribution?

In truth, the meaning of freedom, as formulated in (2), is silent with respect to the distribution that constitutes equality. Accordingly, ethical approval of the market distribution is not defended in Friedman's theory. It is a gratuitous premise. Nor will it help to say that the market distribution is good because a free market assures the most effective or efficient use of resources. For "effective" or "efficient" in this phrase can only mean the best at producing benefits, and, as we have seen, the production of benefits is also a distribution of them. Consequently, the free market is most effective only if its distribution is most appropriate or at least as good as any other.

Friedman is aware of this problem, but his discussion of "the distribution of income" (1962, 161f.) in effect concedes that his liberal theory begs the question. He argues that some of the disparities of income in a market society reflect "equalizing differences" and, in any case, that market societies have, historically speaking, led to greater equality than any alternative system. But he recognizes that these considerations do not settle the matter. In market societies there is considerable inequality that "reflects initial differences in endowment, both of human capacities and of property," and "this is the part that raises the really difficult ethical issue" (1962, 163–64). He then concludes that the market distribution "cannot in and of itself be regarded as an ethical principle; it must be regarded as instrumental or a corollary of some other principle such as freedom" (1962, 165). But what does freedom mean here? If it means voluntary exchange *given* the market distribution, the line of thought is obviously circular. If it means voluntary exchange given some other distribution, then the market distribution would not be a corollary of it.

Nor does it help when Friedman affirms "equality of opportunity" as opposed to "equality of outcome," thereby suggesting that the former provides the justification for the market distribution. Equality of opportunity means that "no arbitrary obstacles should prevent people from achieving those positions for which their talents fit them and which their values lead them to seek" (1980, 132). This leads him to assert that "birth, nationality, color, religion, sex" are morally irrelevant to the opportunities society permits, and he reaffirms that all persons have a right to education (1980, 132). But he also notes that pursuit of one's values is "subject . . . to the agreement of other parties to the transaction," or subject to the conditions of voluntary exchange itself (1980, 133). With the introduction of these conditions, the question of distribution is again avoided, because it becomes clear that equality of opportunity means, for Friedman, opportunity within the free-market system. But, as we have seen, it is precisely the opportunities provided by the market distribution whose equality requires justification. In what *equality* of opportunity consists is the very question at issue, and Friedman's suggestion that the market is consistent with such equality is based upon an assumption regarding the very thing that needs to be defended.

It should be emphasized that someone who rejects the market distribution—in the name, say, of some other meaning of equality—does not have to sacrifice the principle of freedom. Rather, one could change the *meaning* of freedom and thereby specify differently when it is that one is coerced or in what sense it can be said that individuals have an equal right to satisfy their wants. Friedman's understanding of coercion assumes the market distribution. If, to the contrary, one insisted upon some other distribution, it could properly be said that individuals are coerced when the social system so distributes benefits as to deprive them of their rightful amounts. To put the matter in Friedman's terms, market exchanges always have the following, massive neighborhood effect—they affect the distribution of benefits, and this distribution could be at variance with the principle of freedom because it coerces some into a situation that violates their equal right to want-satisfaction. The meaning of freedom, in other words, waits upon an affirmation about distribution. This, I take it, is what Charles E. Lindblom means in saying: "The traditional liberal argument is incomplete unless it defends private property as itself consistent with freedom, a point on which it is silent" (Lindblom, 46). Friedman's silence on this point is evident in the following: "The equalitarian . . . will defend taking from some to give to others . . . on the grounds of 'justice.' At this point, equality comes sharply into conflict with freedom [i.e., Friedman's specification of freedom]; one must choose. One cannot be both an egalitarian, in this sense, and a liberal" (1962, 195). It is clear which Friedman has chosen. It is equally clear that he has not given his choice a reasoned defense.

I conclude that from (1) humans seek satisfaction of wants that are solely preferential; and (2) each individual should be free, that is, has an equal right, to satisfy his or her wants; it does not follow that (3) free market relationships should be maximized. Friedman may respond that equalitarianism, in the sense just discussed, also does not follow. Given (1) and (2), at least for all Friedman has told us, it is true that "one must choose," and this is because the meaning of freedom in the second assertion waits upon rather than provides a principle of distribution. In other words, divergent distributional principles could be substituted for Friedman's affirmation of the competitive market without loss of consistency, but no grounds have been advanced upon which the contention among these principles might be adjudicated. It follows, then, that (2), at least as Friedman understands it, is false. Just because this understanding of freedom is indeterminate in the absence of an independent standard of distribution, freedom cannot be the "ultimate goal in judging social arrangements." In sum, Friedman's theory of associations is incoherent. The principle asserted to be fundamental both requires and, because it is fundamental, does not permit another principle without which the meaning of the first is indeterminate. It is this incoherence which makes Friedman's argument for competitive capitalism a non sequitur.

But freedom is said to be the "ultimate goal" because (1) humans seek to satisfy solely preferential wants. Thus, we may also say that Friedman's fundamental problem is directly related to his affirmation of the established liberal view of happiness. Another established liberal theory might contend that the affirmation of (1) does not necessarily commit one to Friedman's formulation of (2). But Friedman clearly believes the contrary, and, at least in that sense, the incoherence involved in (2) is directly related to (1).

Still, the proposal that Friedman may have incorrectly derived (2) from (1), so that (1) is possibly true, leads one to ask whether he offers any convincing reasons for affirming the preferential view of self-interest. Unfortunately, Friedman is also silent on this matter. Indeed, in this case, he gives no evidence that the claim should be considered debatable. On the contrary, he apparently takes the established liberal view to be more or less self-evident, at least in the sense that it stands beyond serious controversy. Thereby, he writes political theory as if it were more or less obviously a part or extension of neoclassical economics, in accord with which consumer preferences must be taken as given, so that his theory also illustrates the wedding between political liberalism and modern economics that was effected in the nineteenth century.

But the preferential view of happiness is hardly self-evident. Many political philosophers have held to the contrary, and a case might be made that the preferential view is virtually peculiar to modern established liberal theory. Most alternatives in Western philosophy, informed by classical Greek or Christian traditions, have asserted that certain things ought to be wanted or pursued and others shunned. Distinctions have been drawn between human and bestial pursuits, or between conformity to and violation of God's will. Friedman might respond that these distinctions among wants belong to the realm of "individual ethics and philosophy" (1962, 12). But this response misses the point. In saying this, he means that these distinctions are left to individual decision, such that there is no objective moral criterion in accord with which they may be drawn. Were this not the case, the distinctions could not be independent of political theory. The point is that alternative political traditions have asserted an objective standard of good or better pursuits, such that political theory cannot be formulated independently of this standard, and in some sense the social order should facilitate the realization of higher or more divine human possibilities. Friedman may choose, with many other liberals, to say that human self-interests are solely matters of preference. But he has given no reason why the rest of us should follow him in that choice, no reason, that is, why we should affirm (1).

Moreover, Friedman's affirmation that wants are solely preferential involves an apparent problem. Just because the preferential view excludes an ethical criterion in accord with which the good for an individual is defined, self-interests are neither good nor bad in a moral sense. But can one consistently assert a normative or moral theory of human activity and simultaneously assert that the ends or self-interests for the sake of which activity is undertaken are themselves nonmoral? The issue here is not the more familiar one of whether moral claims make sense if one simultaneously claims that human activity as such is egoistic. For Friedman, the self-interests for which one acts may not be one's own, or at least not exclusively one's own. When an individual acts in accord with the principle of freedom, although an exercise of coercion is possible and would enhance his or her benefit, the interests of others are also served, and the matter is, perhaps, all the clearer when one engages in charity. The present issue is whether a moral principle can be consistently advanced when the purposes in terms of which it is defined, whether those of self or others, are solely preferential. Friedman's theory rests upon the claim that human relationships may be moral or immoral even though the interests without which human relationships would be pointless are neither the one nor the other. I noted earlier that the principle of freedom is, in Friedman's theory, negatively defined (freedom is the absence of coercion) and that the corresponding positive claim is that humans seek to satisfy wants. The problem is whether the absence of coercion can be moral when the corresponding presence cannot be, when wants are not positive in a moral sense.

It might be said that Friedman's understanding of freedom is not in fact sheerly negative. Mutually voluntary relations necessarily participate in the democratic state and are necessarily informed. Accordingly, freedom means or at least involves the presence of the state and of education. Similarly, one might say that "effective freedom" implies or requires, as I suggested in the discussion of charity, a certain minimal level of property. But this qualification does not remove the apparent problem. For the prerequisites of state, education, and property properly define the absence of coercion, such that they do not constitute the corresponding positive. On the contrary, they are prescribed for the sake of satisfying wants that are solely preferential. A given human activity is moral or immoral only in the respect that it minimizes or intends to minimize coercion, but its inclusive purpose, which is always to satisfy wants, is nonmoral. Thus, the activity may be in part moral although inclusively or as a whole it cannot be moral.

I suggest that this claim is involved in an apparent fallacy that I will call the "partialist fallacy" and that may be clarified by analogous statements concerning existence. It is, I take it, fallacious to assert that human activities can exist in part but never as wholes. If activities as wholes cannot exist, then neither can parts of activities, at least not as parts *of those activities*. Predications of morality are apparently similar. If human activities as wholes cannot be moral, neither can parts of them, and assertions to the contrary are fallacious. At this point in the inquiry, I will leave discussion of this apparent fallacy with the more or less intuitive appeal upon which it has depended. One cannot clearly establish that such a claim is fallacious (and thereby establish that the analogy with existential statements is instructive) without a constructive argument regarding moral evaluation. The principal intent of chapter 4 is to present just such a constructive argument, the conclusion of which is that moral evaluation prescribes for human activity comprehensively. Here I mean simply to suggest that an incoherence in Friedman's theory might be expected, because he affirms the established liberal view of happiness.

Friedman might seek to escape from this apparent fallacy by insisting that his affirmation of human want-satisfaction has been misunderstood. It does not mean that self-interests are neither good nor bad, he might say, but rather that all human wants are, in a moral sense, *equally good*. Accordingly, self-interest is a matter of preference, in the sense that there is no moral choice among possible wants, but it is not, as I have put it, *solely* a matter of preference, because satisfaction of some want rather than none at all is objectively good. It follows that want-satisfaction as such is intrinsically good, and it is this to which free human relationships are instrumental. Attractive as this formulation may appear, however, it will not withstand examination. The claim that all wants are equally good implicitly introduces another moral principle into Friedman's theory, a principle that defines the character of good things in such a way that all of the possible things which humans might want are instances of that character—and equally so. Further, this claim implies that singular wants or "want units" may be discriminated, such that the things which are equal in goodness are identifiable. Is the want for a two-week vacation a single want or many wants, equal or unequal to the want for a new car? That these two conditions may be met, i.e., that the good may be so defined and singular wants so identified that all of the latter are equal instances of the former, appears on its face a highly implausible claim. But the case against it is far stronger, for success in meeting those conditions would be self-defeating, would deny the conclusion that self-interest is a matter of preference. Just because want-satisfaction is objectively good, it will be better to satisfy more want units rather than less, and the self-interest of each individual will be defined as satisfaction of the largest possible number of objectively identifiable singular wants. Since wants are not always compossible (choosing one now will sometimes preclude choosing another later), it will be better to choose wants which maximize the want units that might be pursued overall. In this way, a distinction between genuine and putative self-interest will have been introduced. I conclude that self-interest can be a matter of preference only if it is solely a matter of preference, so that Friedman's theory does not permit a moral criterion by virtue of which the good for an individual is defined.

Enough has been said to justify the claim that Friedman does not offer a convincing political theory or, therefore, a convincing perspective on independent associations. The principle of freedom, by which the theory is informed, is said to be supreme and yet begs for an independent principle in accord with which proper distribution might be defined. Since, at least according to Friedman, freedom is supreme because humans seek to satisfy solely preferential wants, we may say that the problems in this theory are directly related to his version of the established liberal view of happiness. There is, as a consequence, sufficient reason to explore other theories of associations.

Three

Twentieth-Century Established Liberalism

Alan Gewirth

The theory of Alan Gewirth will be reviewed in this chapter as an illustration of twentieth-century established liberalism. Of course, the claim that Gewirth's thought serves this purpose can be discussed only subsequent to a presentation of his achievement. In the meantime, there is no recent ethical or political theory that is argued with more precision, clarity and completeness than his. If there are problems in Gewirth's position, the reader is likely to discover them only because the author tenaciously pursues the logic of his claims and entertains every objection he can muster to every step in that pursuit. Accordingly, if this theory is the illustration that I claim it to be, there is none other that will better serve the purpose for which it is chosen.

For Gewirth, a theory of associations is explicitly and systematically an application of moral theory. In order to know how humans ought to act in association, one must first know how humans ought to act. Gewirth's major work to date, *Reason and Morality* (1978; all subsequent page references in this chapter are to this volume), is principally an attempt to address the logically prior problem, and he notes in the Preface that sociopolitical issues will be dealt with more fully in a sequel volume. Nonetheless, the closing chapter of the present work constitutes a considerable beginning on the task of applying his moral philosophy to these issues, and from it alone one can formulate an implied perspective on independent associations.

The Principle of Generic Consistency

A reading of Gewirth's associational theory must wait upon an understanding of his solution to "the most important and difficult problem of philosophical ethics" (ix). The venture is a bold one. Gewirth claims to succeed where a long tradition in Western philosophy has nobly failed, namely, in giving a rational justification for a moral principle that is both supreme and substantial. In presenting a *rational justification*, Gewirth means to avoid ethical intuitionism, according to which moral rules or principles are self-evident or known to be true upon direct inspection. In presenting a moral principle that is *supreme* (a principle whose requirements "cannot rightly be evaded by any action or institution" [23; see also 158], such that every other principle or rule to which actions and institutions are morally obligated must be justified by this principle), Gewirth means to avoid ethical "relativism," according to which all moral principles derive from culture, tradition, social system, or some other variable feature of the human condition. In presenting a supreme principle that is *substantial*, Gewirth means to avoid ethical "formalism," according to which agents are required to universalize their judgments, but the content to be universalized is relative to the variable interests or decisions of the agents.

Gewirth proposes to solve the most difficult problem in philosophical ethics "by applying reason to the concept of action" (22). Indeed, "the chief novelty" in Gewirth's approach to the problem "is the logical derivation of a substantial normative principle from the nature of human action" (x). By implication, this same novelty makes it possible for him to succeed where so many others have failed. Beginning with the concept of action, Gewirth emphasizes, does not make the argument persuasive in the sense of presupposing some moral position. On the contrary, the concept is "morally neutral," because "it fits all moralities rather than reflecting or deriving from any one normative moral position as against any other" (25). Moreover, the relevant meaning of "action" is that common to the whole field of practice, and is therefore the common object of all other practical precepts (e.g., technical, prudential, aesthetic) as well as moral ones, so that this beginning does not even presuppose that any moral precepts can be rationally justified. Whatever can be logically derived from the concept of action can be logically avoided "only by disavowing and refraining from . . . the whole sphere of practice" (29).

If this concept is to constitute the basis for an argument, there must be some necessary content to action as such, so that the concept indeed has some univocal meaning. Gewirth calls this necessary content the "generic features" of action. He argues that these features may be specified by examining what the objects of practical precepts have in common. All practical precepts, he continues, "guide, advise, or urge" people to fashion their behavior reflectively in accord with those precepts (26). But this makes sense only if "the hearers can control their behavior through their unforced choice so as to try to achieve the prescribed ends or contents" (26–27). He concludes that *voluntariness* and *purposiveness* are the generic features of action. Both of these features are analyzed at some length, but in the present context it is sufficient to say that actions are voluntary in being the result of "unforced and informed choice" (31) and purposive in the sense of having some desired or intended goal or content (37), although it is important to note that this goal need not be constiuted by anything beyond the action itself. Both generic features may be either occurrent or dispositional, i.e., may describe some character of the specific action itself or some more enduring characteristic of the agent of which the specific action is a consequence or specification. In the former case, one is more or less immediately reflective about the action in question; in the latter case, the action is more or less habitual, although not for that reason beyond the agent's control. Moreover, because the features of agency as such may be dispositional, one need not be immediately active in order to be an agent. One may be a "prospective agent" (see, e.g., 62) in the sense that one has the capacity for, and holds open the possibility of, becoming an agent when one so chooses. Voluntariness and purposiveness, Gewirth insists, exhaust the generic characteristics of action. "Voluntariness refers to the means, purposiveness to the end" (41). "Intention or purpose, in the sense of the desired content of an action, is the other side of the control and choice that constitute voluntariness or freedom and that are concerned with bringing about that desired content" (38).

"Once it is determined what constitutes being an agent, the dialectically necessary method takes over" (123). If the argument is unique because it is based upon the concept of action, it is also novel because it proceeds through the "dialectically necessary" method. The method is dialectical in the Aristotelian sense that it begins with certain claims or assumptions and proceeds to examine what these logically imply. It moves, as Gewirth says many times, "from within the standpoint of the agent" (44). It is dialectically necessary because the claims derive from the generic features of action and therefore are necessary claims for any actor qua actor. The claims, and what follows from them, can be logically avoided only if one ceases to be an agent. The argument is basically simple, although this fact does not subtract from, indeed it emphasizes, Gewirth's philosophical sophistication. There are four steps: (1) An actor necessarily claims that the purpose which he or she voluntarily pursues is good. (2) Consequently, an actor necessarily claims that the generic features of his or her action are good. (3) Consequently, an actor necessarily claims rights to generic voluntariness and purposiveness.

(4) Consequently, an actor is logically committed to recognizing that the recipients of his or her action have those same rights. We should examine each of these four steps.

In the first step, Gewirth argues that an actor necessarily claims that the purpose which he or she voluntarily pursues is good. " 'I do X for purpose E.' . . . entails 'E is good' " (49), i.e., "I hold that E is good" or "E seems to me good." This need not mean that the agent reflectively evaluates the particular purpose, although in some sense one does reflectively evaluate at least some larger goal of which the particular purpose is more or less obviously a part (50). Nor need it mean that the particular purpose is a means to something else; the actor may value the action for its own sake (50). Finally, this first step does not imply that the actor evaluates his or her purpose as *morally* good (49–50). There are many nonmoral uses of the term "good," and it is sufficient for the argument that the purpose is seen by the agent as prudentially good, good in terms of the fulfillment of his or her interests. This last indicates that a purpose invariably seems good to the agent simply because it is something wanted or intended and, therefore, something he or she regards "as worth aiming at or pursuing" (49). Gewirth recognizes that some will object to this first step by saying that an agent may want what he or she wants solely because he or she wants it—and that is the end of the matter. To this, he answers: if one did not regard one's purpose to be good, one "would not unforcedly choose to move from quiescence or nonaction to action with a view to achieving the goal" (49). The agent "at least wants to perform some action rather than none" (51), and this conative character to all action implies that the pursuit aims at some good.

Because a particular purpose is always positively evaluated by the agent, Gewirth moves to the second step: an actor necessarily claims that the generic features (voluntariness and purposiveness) of his or her action are good. One might say that the value of the end (the particular purpose) implies the value of the means (the generic features), as long as the means-end category is not confined to strictly instrumental relationships but also includes those in which the means are constitutive aspects of the end. Voluntariness as a generic good needs no explanation. In referring here to generic purposiveness, Gewirth means that an agent "regards as good . . . an increase in his level of purpose-fulfillment" (53), this being inescapably the point of pursuing any goal at all.

Purposiveness includes three dimensions or kinds of good—basic, nonsubtractive, and additive—each of which has both a particular and generic meaning. In their particular meanings, they are relative to each person; in their generic meanings, they refer to conditions or capabilities "required for fulfilling . . . purposes" that "are the same for all persons" (59). Thus, for instance, "basic goods" refers to "necessary preconditions of action" (54) which, generally speaking, include "life and physical integrity . . . mental equilibrium and a feeling of confidence as to the general possibility of attaining one's goals" (54). In the fully particular sense of the term, heated shelter is probably a basic good for someone living in Nova Scotia but the heat need not be included for someone living in Haiti. "Non-subtractive goods," in the particular sense, refers to nonbasic things that an agent already has and considers good, such that it is part of the agent's purpose to maintain them. Certain properties or relationships are, in certain cases, examples. Generically speaking, the term refers to those universal capabilities of action without which purposeful retention of goods is at least compromised. Such general capacities require, Gewirth illustrates, that one is not "lied to, cheated, stolen from, defamed, [or] insulted"; is not the victim of broken promises or violations of privacy; or is not subject to "dangerous, degrading, or excessively debilitating conditions of physical labor or housing or other strategic situations of life when resources are available for improvement" (233). "Additive goods," to complete the trio, refers in its particular sense to anything an agent wants to "add" to his or her goods, any "positive object of any purpose" (56) that is not a basic or nonsubtractive good of the agent in question. Generically speaking, the term refers to capabilities of action that are neither basic nor nonsubtractive and that are universally required for an agent to increase his or her level of purpose-fulfillment. Central among these, Gewirth says, "is the prospective agent's sense of his own worth," without which the achievement of further goals "becomes problematic" (241–42), and "closely related" to which are certain virtues of character (courage, temperance, and prudence) and certain general conditions (freedom, knowledge, education, wealth, and income) (242–43).

We need not pause to examine the examples in detail. It is sufficient in the present context to clarify the fundamental distinctions (between preconditions for action as such, universal capabilities for maintaining achievements considered good, and universal capabilities for increasing achievement) among the kinds of goods included in generic purposiveness. Summarily, Gewirth refers to these goods as the agent's "well-being." Hence, he can say that an agent is logically committed to a positive evaluation of his or her general freedom (or voluntariness) and well-being. In this second step, as in the first, the meaning of "good" is not necessarily moral. The evaluation of one's generic freedom and well-being, as the evaluation of one's particular purposes, may be simply prudential.

Gewirth now moves to the third step in the argument: because an agent necessarily claims that his or her generic freedom and well-being are good, he or she also necessarily claims *generic rights* to these generic conditions of action. "Rights" is here used in a strict sense, such that it entails corresponding duties on the part of other people. That the agent has generic rights means that others ought not to interfere with his or her freedom and well-being. The criteria for this claim are still not necessarily moral; rather, the agent may claim to have *prudential* rights on the grounds that his or her generic conditions of agency are *prudentially* good (71). Why is a claim to generic *rights* entailed? Consider, says Gewirth, the alternative: if the agent fails to claim such rights, then it is permissible for others to interfere with his or her freedom and well-being; but this denies that these generic conditions are necessarily good (78–79). If they are necessarily good, then they are properly protected—that is the point. Alternatively stated: to pursue a purpose is to say, "I ought to do X"; but to reject the claim to generic rights is to say, "It is not true that others ought to refrain from interfering with my freedom and well-being." But freedom and well-being are necessary conditions of doing X, and "one cannot rationally both accept that something ought to be done and reject a necessary condition of its being done" (91). The point, if I understand it rightly, is an application of the dictum, "Ought implies can." If one ought to do X, then one ought to be able to do X.

The stage is now set for the final step in Gewirth's argument, the derivation of a supreme principle of morality. The move is based upon the following formal principle: "Whatever is right for one person must be right for any similar person in similar circumstances" (105). This formal moral principle cannot be consistently denied because it is derived from "a more general logical principle of universalizability" (105). This latter says that if S is P because S is or has Q, where "because" means that Q is a *sufficient* reason for S being P, then any S_1, S_2, etc. that also is or has Q is also P. To deny this is to say that a sufficient reason is not a sufficient reason, which is self-contradictory (105). If one person has a right, then any similar person in similar circumstances has the same right, where "similar person in similar circumstances" means that the conditions which were the *sufficient* reason for the one person having the right are also present with respect to the others.

Everything turns, then, on "the criterion of relevant similarities." How does one know when others are similar people in similar circumstances? Given what has been said, this question may be translated: what is the sufficient reason for the one person having the right? With reference to the generic rights, the answer is clear. An agent claims generic rights to freedom and well-being solely by virtue of being an agent; agency as such necessarily entails this claim by the agent. By the principle of universalizability, the agent is logically bound to claim that all prospective agents who are recipients of his or her action have the same rights. Upon pain of contradiction, every agent is bound to the moral Principle of Generic Consistency (the PGC): "Act in accord with the generic rights of your recipients as well as of yourself" (135).

This, finally, is a *moral* claim, for Gewirth means by a morality "a set of categorically obligatory requirements for action that are addressed at least in part to every actual or prospective agent, and that are concerned with furthering the interests, especially the most important interests, of persons or recipients other than or in addition to the agent or the speaker" (1). Because the PGC requires that the agent be concerned with furthering the interests of others, it is a moral principle—even though it is derived from rights claimed by the agent that were, in the first instance at least, prudential in character. Negatively, the PGC requires that the agent "refrain from coercing and from harming the recipients" and positively that he or she "assist them to have freedom and well-being whenever they cannot otherwise have these necessary goods and he can help them at no comparable cost to himself" (135).

The PGC is an egalitarian universalist moral principle (140), because it *equally* affirms the generic rights to action of *all* agents. It is also, as Gewirth takes pains throughout the volume to insist, a "deontological" rather than "utilitarian" or "consequentialist" or "aggregative" principle. This distinction has been used and discussed by many twentieth-century moral philosophers, and the meanings of the terms have not always been constant. For Gewirth, however, its importance consists in emphasizing that the PGC is primarily attentive to the *distribution of rights*, not to the *maximization of some aggregate* (e.g., utility or happiness). "The PGC requires that the agent not distribute the necessary goods of freedom and well-being in a way that is disadvantageous to his recipients" (330). Finally, it is worth noting, as Gewirth does, that the argument begins with the empirical assertion that an agent acts for purposes and it concludes with a supreme moral principle. Thus, the argument shows how to derive "ought" from "is" (149).

Associations

We have now learned how humans ought to act (in accord with the Principle of Generic Consistency) and why they ought to act in this way. Thus, we are prepared for a discussion of how humans ought to act in associations, i.e., for a theory of associations. This discussion involves, in Gewirth's terms, indirect applications of the PGC. The social rules of associations or institutions are justified by the PGC and, in turn, the actions of individuals are regulated by these social rules. The social rules are intermediate between the PGC and individual actors, so that the application of the principle to action is indirect (272).

The significance of distinguishing between direct and indirect applications of the principle can be appreciated by attending to one of Gewirth's favorite examples. According to social rules of criminal justice that are justified by the PGC, a judge may impose upon a convicted criminal a sentence that deprives the defendant of his or her freedom. Were the PGC applied directly to the transaction between judge and defendant, it would be violated by the judge's action. Because it is applied indirectly, the action is morally proper. The meaning of indirect applications of the PGC may also be stated in terms of the "criterion of relevant similarities." Where direct applications of the principle are concerned, one must not coerce or harm recipients, because they are relevantly similar in the quality by virtue of which one claims rights to generic freedom and well-being—namely, in being prospective agents. Where justified social rules apply, however, the relevant quality determining rights "is no longer the generic quality of being a prospective purposive agent" (278) but now the more specific quality defined by the role one plays or occupies in the institution. Thus, the judge may coerce the convicted defendant precisely because they are relevantly dissimilar—one is a judge and the other is a criminal.

Some might ask why it is morally proper, in this or any similar case, to apply the PGC indirectly. Such a question could have two different meanings. First, it might be the complete anarchist's question: why ought humans to form associations; or, more precisely, why is it even morally *permissible* for humans to form associations? On the one hand, Gewirth does not have a great deal of patience with this question. "To be human is to engage in action and in association. . . . It would be as pointless to ask whether the PGC justifies there being any social rules or institutions in general as it would be to seek from the PGC (or any other moral principle) a justification for persons' performing actions at all" (278). On the other hand, as we shall see, he tries to show why the PGC not only permits some social rules but also why it makes others morally necessary.

But, second, the question about indirect applications may ask why the requirements of morally justified institutions should take *precedence* over direct applications of the PGC? Gewirth answers that only this relation is consistent with there being any associations at all. Institutional rules "define what persons are required to do if they are to participate in the respective activities or functions; and these requirements are the obligations persons have qua such participants" (274). If, to the contrary, direct applications took precedence over indirect, or if the matter were morally indifferent, then the social rules constituting justified institutions would not be rules at all since one would be obligated to obey them only when they were consistent with direct applications of the PGC. Thus, justified social rules "take precedence in the relevant social contexts over the PGC's direct applications, because the latter deal primarily with transactions among individuals that do not fall within contexts structured according to these rules" (277).

We turn, then, to the grounds upon which social rules or institutions are justified. We have seen that action has the generic features of voluntariness and purposiveness, where "voluntariness refers to the means, purposiveness to the end" (41). As a result, the PGC mandates equality of generic rights to freedom and well-being. Correspondingly, says Gewirth, there are two ways in which institutions are justified: (1) when the means by which they are constituted are "in accord with persons' rights to freedom" (282), and (2) when the ends which they serve "protect and extend well-being" (281). (In this last formulation, Gewirth includes freedom as an aspect of well-being, so that it may be more precise to say that institutions are justified when the ends which they serve protect and extend the equality of generic rights.) Gewirth calls these two sorts of justification "procedural" and "instrumental," respectively. The relations between the two are, as we shall see, complex, but, generally speaking, both moral means and moral ends are required unless some reason to the contrary is itself justified by the PGC. The matter is further complicated because both procedural and instrumental justifications come in two forms. Procedural justifications may be optional or necessary, instrumental justifications may be static or dynamic. I will now try to clarify each of these four forms.

Let us begin with the instrumental justifications. Because the equality of generic rights is a moral rather than empirical principle, equal rights may in fact be violated. Social rules are instrumentally justified when they protect and extend this equality. The static-instrumental justification refers to social rules that seek to protect or restore an assumed actual equality that might be or has been intentionally violated (292). The principal illustrations of rules so justified are those of the criminal law. In a simplified paradigm: when one person acts in violation of another's generic rights (for instance, through killing, kidnapping, physically assaulting, robbing, or defaming the second), the criminal law serves to restore the "original equality" by preventing the violator "from profiting through his violation" and, where possible, through coercing restitution (297). In addition, the rules of criminal law serve to protect the assumed equality of rights by having a deterrent effect. "By calling to public notice the punishment and the threat thereof, the rules are intended to bring it about that persons refrain from inflicting on others the basic and other serious harms the PGC prohibits" (299). Institutions of the criminal law that are justified in the static-instrumental way are called by Gewirth "the minimal state."

In the dynamic-instrumental justification, actual equality of rights is not assumed. Rather, this form "recognizes that persons are . . . unequal in their actual ability to attain and protect their generic rights, especially their rights to basic well-being, and it provides that social rules are justified when they serve to remove this inequality" (292). People who suffer economic and certain other privations, when the want is not the result of and cannot be remedied by their own voluntary action, "do not have effective rights to well-being" (312). Thus, the PGC justifies certain institutions that seek to redistribute aspects of generic well-being, such as income or opportunities for education (314). Gewirth emphasizes, however, that the aim of such redistributive social rules is "meliorative rather than . . . revolutionary" (312). Inequality of generic goods is not always the result of circumstances beyond the control of the people involved. Rewards based upon voluntary effort and accomplishment, as well as situations attendant upon the absence of effort, are morally justified. This follows, Gewirth holds, from the right freely to pursue one's purposes. The PGC requires protection of the agent's rights as well as those of the recipients. The agent is positively required to help recipients only when "they cannot otherwise have these necessary goods and he can help them at no comparable cost to himself" (135). In addition to redistributive institutions, the dynamic-instrumental justification also calls for institutions that provide certain public goods (for instance, unpolluted air, public safety, protection against fire) that are "common" in the sense that they are goods "had by each person" (211). These institutions, like redistributive ones, do not assume an actual inequality of rights; on the contrary, the assumption is that the absence of such institutions would, by sheer force of disorderly circumstance, lead to an inequality in the goods that they help make common. The primary illustrations justified in the dynamic-instrumental way are called by Gewirth "the supportive state" (312).

I have mentioned the state with respect to both static-instrumental and dynamic-instrumental forms of justification. It is time to see what this term means and why instrumental justifications lead to it. Gewirth's notion of the state is, as is Friedman's, the traditional one of an association to which all individuals within a society (or within a certain territory) must belong. The state, generally speaking, is not only morally permissible but morally required because "among multitudes of persons living together, there must be uniform rules" (305), obedience to which is obligatory for all members of the society. These rules (or laws) are, therefore, coercive "in that their claim to obedience is backed by a threat of punishment for noncompliance" (305). Uniform rules as such are required (and, consequently, the state as such is justified) by the PGC because, in their absence, "there will be disorder and unpredictability, and conflicts of interest will be unresolved or resolved only by force" (305). Consider the situation, for instance, were there no uniform traffic rules. Without the state, in other words, there will be no way to insure equality of generic rights.

That there ought to be a state as such, then, follows directly from the PGC, and its justification is both static- and dynamic-instrumental. Gewirth holds that both the reality and the content of the minimal state (the criminal law) follow directly from the PGC. The state must enforce such laws in order to insure stability and uniformity, and "their content [e.g., laws against murder, theft, defamation] is largely the same as the basic part of the PGC" (300). If this is so, then both the reality and the content of the minimal state is justified solely on the basis of their static-instrumental relation to the PGC. What, then, of the procedural question? These institutions are imposed upon members of society, in that their justification in no way calls for an exercise of the members' freedom or voluntary consent, but freedom is one of the generic rights to be protected. Gewirth's answer is that the minimal state no more contradicts the right to freedom than does the PGC itself. Since the minimal state is mandated by the PGC (i.e., is morally necessary), it has the "rational consent" of members of the society, just as they are rationally or logically bound to the supreme moral principle itself.

The reality of the supportive state is also morally necessary. Private individuals who are willing to do so may help with the required redistribution of generic goods and the provision of public goods, but "it is plausible to hold that the primary responsibility must rest with the state" (315). Only the state can insure that the needed arrangements are securely provided, that the benefits are impartially distributed, and that the costs are assessed in proportion to ability (315). The content of the supportive state is another matter. These laws are "concerned with more ongoing, particular problems" and with "complex issues" that "involve conflicts of opinion and interest in the society whose just treatment requires more circumstantial, detailed inquiry" (321). That there are some or other laws of this kind (and some or other public officials to make and enforce them) is morally necessary; the specificity is morally contingent. Gewirth relates the two by saying that the PGC mandates a certain kind of constitution which defines a decision-making procedure for selecting officials and formulating laws. Since the specificity is morally contingent, it does not have the rational consent of individuals; hence the decision-making process must be one that maximizes equal freedom, consistent with the moral necessity of the supportive state as such. This constitutional procedure Gewirth calls "the method of consent." Central to the method of consent is the equal distribution of civil liberties and the protection of their use in the decision process (307–8). The form of justification of social rules arrived at by the method of consent he calls "necessary-procedural," i.e., there must be some such rules but the particular ones are justified by the procedure.

"Thus, four levels of political objects may be distinguished: (1) the minimal state with the criminal law, (2) the supportive state with its need for other laws and officials, (3) its constitutional structure providing for certain consensual decision-procedures, (4) the specific laws and officials determined by the use of these procedures" (306). The first three are justified solely instrumentally (the first by the static-instrumental form; the second and third by the dynamic-instrumental form), because they are morally necessary and are the objects of rational consent. The fourth is justified by the necessary-procedural form and is the object of the method of consent.

The final form of justification for indirect application of the PGC is optional-procedural, and with this we arrive at a consideration of voluntary associations. These associations are moral because "participants voluntarily or optionally consent to participate and hence to be subject to the rules" (286), where "voluntary" means, as it always does for Gewirth, that choices are "unforced" and are made with "knowledge of relevant circumstances, and a certain degree of emotional calm" (284). Thus, the constraints are "in an important respect, . . . self-imposed" (286). In contrast to the supportive state, no voluntary association is morally *necessary*. There is no moral requirement that participants should consent to the rules, no requirement that there be participants. Rather these associations are morally *permissible*, moral if people so consent. A voluntary association is an extension of the generic right to freedom. Participants have freely agreed for purposes of their own to have their actions qua participants obligated to the rules of the association. It would be contradictory, Gewirth argues, to deny the moral permissibility of these organizations. For to deny that "all persons have a . . . right to participate in activities or associations whose rules they have freely accepted" is inconsistent with "all prospective purposive agents have a right to freedom," and the latter is included in the PGC (286). To say that voluntary consent justifies an association does not mean that its purposes are morally irrelevant. More precisely, Gewirth says that voluntary associations are prima facie morally permissible, where this means that their moral justification can be overridden by other moral considerations deriving from the PGC. A robber gang may be freely constituted, but, because it exists to coerce or harm nonmembers, it is immoral. A voluntary association is permissible, then, if it is instrumentally consistent with the PGC—if its purposes do not violate the equality of generic rights.

From what has been said, it might seem that Gewirth holds all justifiable nongovernmental organizations to be voluntary associations. On the contrary, however, he says that "there is much unrealism in the distinction sometimes drawn between 'public' and 'private' associations, with the former being classed as 'compulsory' and the latter as 'voluntary'" (289). Specifically, he notes that "insofar as membership in various professional organizations, labor unions, and other interest groups is a necessary condition of earning a livelihood, such membership may reflect a kind of forced choice on the part of persons who want to pursue the relevant profession, trade or business" (289). The same might be said regarding the positions of employment that many people accept. But this kind of forced choice does not necessarily mean that these nongovernmental organizations are immoral. They may be instrumentally justified; they may so contribute to the well-being of their members and thus to the equality of generic rights as to make the "forced choice" right. What this implies is that voluntariness of association is a matter of degree, and at some point it is no longer proper to call a nongovernmental organization a voluntary association.

It may be helpful to summarize the indirect application of the PGC schematically, as in figure 2. This figure shows the basic distinctions among associations that are significant from the perspective of Gewirth's moral theory. The figure is also designed to show clearly the difference between governmental and nongovernmental sectors, in order that we might move to a discussion of independent associations. The one aspect of figure 2 that requires further explanation is the appearance of voluntary associations under the rubric of dynamic-instrumental justification as well as under the rubric of optional-procedural justification. The warrant for this is Gewirth's statement, noted above, that willing private individuals may be helpful with those purposes (the redistribution of generic goods and the provision of public goods) principally assigned to the supportive state. This point will be pursued in the discussion of independent associations that follows.

FIGURE 2
INDIRECT APPLICATION OF THE PGC

	Procedural Justifications		Instrumental Justifications	
	Optional	Necessary	Static	Dynamic
Governmental		Constitutional decision-procedures	Minimal state	Supportive state
Nongovernmental	Voluntary Associations			Forced-choice institutions and Voluntary associations

Other-Regarding Associations

We are now in a position to seek the implications of Gewirth's theory regarding independent associations, a theoretically significant class of institutions that does not include commonplace American examples of governmental or commercial associations, or their equivalents. In this pursuit, we need not pause long over the difference between governmental and nongovernmental classes. The former is inclusive of organizations which define and enforce social rules that are morally obligatory for all members of the society in question, and the distinction between these and all others is significant because the state, in both its minimal and supportive aspects, is, for theoretical reasons, morally necessary. Defining independent institutions remains problematic, however, because nothing has been said explicitly regarding a distinction within the nongovernmental class between commercial and noncommercial associations. In this respect, then, the present discussion must pursue the implicit formulation in Gewirth's theory.

We have seen that institutions may be justified procedurally and/or instrumentally. Although procedural justifications may be optional or necessary, necessary procedural justification applies only to the constitutional decision-procedures of the state. Accordingly, nongovernmental associations are procedurally justified only by virtue of being voluntary. It is clear, however, that voluntariness cannot serve to identify a class of independent associations, because commonplace American examples of commercial organizations may also be voluntary. This conclusion shifts our attention to instrumental justifications, whereby institutions are justified because of their contribution to the equality of generic rights and, therefore, by their provision of basic, nonsubtractive and additive goods. It is important to emphasize that the goods in question must be generic. Some associations, in other words, may be instrumental to a great diversity of nongeneric goods, and in that way be morally permissible, but such associations are procedurally justified, by virtue of their voluntariness. It is also clear that the provision of generic goods cannot serve to identify a class of independent associations, because commonplace examples of American commercial institutions may be instrumentally justified. This is immediately apparent with respect to basic goods, since the provision of a livelihood is one aspect of basic well-being. It may also be argued that ready examples of commercial organizations provide nonsubtractive and additive generic goods. Gewirth contends that nonsubtractive well-being implies that one is not subject to "dangerous, degrading, or excessively debilitating conditions of physical labor or housing or other strategic situations of life when resources are available for improvement" (233), and he says that "wealth and income" are among the general conditions required for additive well-being (243).

It follows from these considerations that Gewirth's theory yields a significant class of independent institutions only if there is a theoretically significant distinction within the class of associations that are instrumental to generic goods. Such a distinction, I suggest, is implied in the fact that the PGC has both *negative* and *positive* requirements. Negatively, it will be recalled, agents ought to refrain from coercing or harming recipients; positively, agents ought to assist recipients to have generic goods whenever the recipients cannot otherwise have those goods and agents can help at no comparable cost to themselves. In accord with the negative requirements, we may conceive of institutions wherein members associate each for the purpose of providing his or her own generic goods and do so without violating or harming recipients. These institutions are constituted by exchange with respect to generic goods, as could be the case, for instance, in an American profit-seeking organization. Such activity may be fully justifiable, and we may call these "self-regarding associations." This class is, incidentally, not necessarily exhausted by commonplace American commercial institutions. Certain community organizations, for instance, would be included.

Nonetheless, there is another class of nongovernmental associations that are instrumental to generic goods. These are institutions wherein members (or at least a significant number thereof) associate in accord with the positive requirements of the PGC, i.e., in order to provide generic goods to recipients because these recipients cannot otherwise have these goods and members of the associations can help at no comparable cost to themselves. We may call these "other-regarding associations." Charitable and social-service organizations, civil rights organizations, and environmental law organizations (which are designed to protect the environment as a public good) are all examples.

It should be emphasized that the distinction between self-regarding and other-regarding associations is not theoretically significant with respect to *all* nongovernmental organizations. As I have noted, institutions whose justification is solely procedural are instrumental to a wide variety of *nongeneric* goods. Because these goods are morally permissible but not required, morality is indifferent to whose goods they are. The distinction between self-regarding and other-regarding contains, in application to those institutions, no theoretical significance. In application to nongovernmental institutions that are instrumentally justified, however, the distinction *is* significant, because morality is not indifferent to whether the positive as well as negative requirements of the PGC are fulfilled. Given this fact, the important point for present purposes is that commonplace examples of American commercial organizations are never other-regarding. People associate in factories, banks, retail stores, and investment firms in order to serve their own economic enhancement, so that, in relation to generic goods, these institutions are self-regarding. Accordingly, we may say that other-regarding associations constitute a theoretically significant class that is nongovernmental and noncommercial—a class of independent associations.

Among other things, this conclusion implies that the class of nonprofit organizations, commonly thought to be identical with the "third sector," has no theoretical significance for Gewirth, and this is one respect in which his theory contrasts with that of Friedman. The reason for this difference is that, for Gewirth, "profit-seeking" institutions also do not constitute a significant class. The important distinctions among nongovernmental organizations divide those which are instrumental to nongeneric goods from those instrumental to generic goods and, within the latter, self-regarding from other-regarding associations. The difference between profit-seeking and nonprofit cannot plausibly be construed so as to coincide with either of these distinctions. By the same token, the distinction between commercial and noncommercial is insignificant in this theory. Although commercial institutions may be instrumental to nongeneric goods, and may be self-regarding in relation to generic goods, they do not, by any plausible meaning of "commercial," exhaust either class. Of course, this does not prevent all independent associations from being noncommercial. By the same token, all independent associations are nonprofit. Thus, we may say that independent associations are, in the theoretical perspective advanced by Gewirth, a subclass of nonprofit organizations, significantly identified as other-regarding.

Nothing that has been said to this point implies, however, that there ought to be independent associations in the social order. It is certainly true that there are positive requirements of the PGC and that institutional means for meeting those requirements are in some measure necessary. But the protection and extension of equal generic rights is primarily assigned to the state, because only the state can fully secure this equality in a way that is consistent with the PGC, and there is no reason in principle why the state alone should not execute the task. Still, willing private individuals may be helpful with those purposes principally assigned to the state and, wherever individuals associate to do so, they constitute a morally significant class of associations. In this respect, then, independent associations are, in Gewirth's theory, similar to those in Friedman's; they constitute a class of theoretically significant, although not morally required, associations.

In the process of clarifying this point, the discussion has also suggested a distinction within the class of other-regarding associations. Since there is a significant distinction between governmental and nongovernmental activity, one might also distinguish theoretically between independent associations that facilitate participation in the constitutional decision-making procedures of the state and those that serve equal generic rights by service to individuals or to other nongovernmental organizations. We may call these political and nonpolitical other-regarding associations respectively. Public-interest law firms are primarily political other-regarding associations; most social-service organizations are primarily nonpolitical other-regarding associations.

The significant distinctions within the social order that are explicit or implicit in Gewirth's theory are summarized schematically in figure 3. It should be apparent from what has been said that a given association may belong to more than one of these significant classes of associations. A given commercial association, for instance, may be a voluntary association and, insofar, procedurally justified. In some measure, however, the institution may also be instrumentally justified as a self-regarding institution, precisely to the extent that it provides for its members the income requisite to well-being. This circumstance has interesting implications for independent associations, as I will now explain.

FIGURE 3
ASSOCIATIONS

<table>
<tr><td></td><td colspan="2">Procedural Justifications</td><td colspan="4">Instrumental Justifications</td></tr>
<tr><td></td><td>Optional</td><td>Necessary</td><td>Static</td><td colspan="3">Dynamic</td></tr>
<tr><td>Governmental</td><td></td><td></td><td></td><td colspan="3"></td></tr>
<tr><td rowspan="2">Nongovernmental</td><td rowspan="2"></td><td rowspan="2"></td><td rowspan="2"></td><td>Self-regarding</td><td colspan="2">Other-regarding</td></tr>
<tr><td></td><td>Nonpolitical</td><td>Political</td></tr>
</table>

In the previous chapter, I argued that Friedman's theory implies a class of nonprofit or independent associations exclusive of many institutions which are commonly included within the "third sector," especially cultural and higher educational institutions, many health-delivery organizations and many religious communities. Such limitations are imposed upon the class because, for Friedman, the principle of equal freedom implies that nonprofit organizations, as governmental activity, are subservient to the free market, in the sense that competitive, profit-seeking relationships should occur wherever possible. In contrast, Gewirth's theory permits a far less circumscribed class of independent associations. Because his normative principle prescribes equal freedom and well-being, governmental activity designed to protect and extend this equality may be considerably more extensive, as witnessed by his discussion of the supportive state. For the same reason, other-regarding associations may be more extensive and diverse. Indeed, just because the generic goods include not only basic but also nonsubtractive and additive goods, there is reason to include among independent associations most nonprofit health-delivery institutions, higher educational, and religious associations. Moreover, if aesthetic sensibility could be considered a general additive good or a general condition therefor, many cultural institutions may also be assigned to this class.

Still, Gewirth's formulation implies limitations upon the independent sector that are at odds with the common understanding. At some point, one might argue, other-regarding associations in pursuit of knowledge, aesthetic sensibility, or religious faith are no longer instrumental to generic goods. However important increases in these goods may be to the capacities for actions as such, there is a point after which the goods cease principally to serve this purpose and are pursued principally for their own sake; they become the particular and morally permissible wants or purposes for which individuals seek to use their generic capacities. An analogy is offered by the pursuit of income in a justified self-regarding institution. Although income is, in some measure, a part of basic well-being and, in further measure, a part of additive well-being, at some level it becomes simply a morally permissible good. Similarly, most higher educational, cultural, and religious associations are only *in part* instrumental to generic goods, so that they belong to the class of independent associations only in the respect that they are other-regarding in this sense. In contrast to the common understanding of the "third sector," then, it is not nonprofit cultural, educational, or religious purposes as such that make associations independent. For insofar as these purposes do not involve the general capacities for action of the recipient constituency, they aim at nongeneric goods. When that is the case, the distinction between these associations and all other nongovernmental associations, including commercial institutions, is theoretically insignificant.

Critical Discussion

In chapter 1, I distinguished between nineteenth- and twentieth-century established liberalism. Whereas the former prescribes minimal government and maximal independence for individuals and the associations which they voluntarily constitute, the latter extends governmental activity and thereby compromises the independence of voluntary organizations in the name of certain understandings of equality or welfare. Nonetheless, both perspectives belong to established liberalism, because they affirm the preferential view of happiness, in accord with which normative or ethical claims refer solely to the proper relations between various individuals of whose self-interests those claims are logically independent. I have also stated that Gewirth's theory was chosen for review as an example of twentieth-century established liberalism, just as Friedman's thought served to illustrate nineteenth-century established liberalism. It is indeed apparent from the preceding discussion that Gewirth differs from Friedman in accord with the stated differences between these two forms of liberalism. His discussion of the supportive state advocates precisely the extension of governmental activity upon which the difference turns, and the reason for this change is precisely Gewirth's affirmation of equal freedom and well-being in contrast to Friedman's more limited notion of equal freedom. As we have seen, Gewirth's different understanding of equality also yields an understanding of independent associations which is significantly more inclusive than Friedman's. Not so readily apparent, however, is my implied claim that Gewirth's theory includes the preferential view of happiness. The purpose of the following discussion, then, is to show that this is the case and, moreover, to show that this inclusion undermines the dialectically necessary derivation of the PGC.

As used here, the preferential view of happiness excludes a moral criterion in accord with which the good for an individual is defined and, consequently, excludes a distinction between putative and genuine self-interests. This last consequence may raise doubts that Gewirth is properly named an established liberal. In the course of his argument for the PGC, he claims to show that every agent necessarily affirms as good for himself or herself the full range of generic capacities for action (basic, nonsubtractive, and additive), and it might be said that these provide the basis for a distinction between putative and genuine self-interests. Accordingly, agents who take their happiness to exclude freedom from insult, violations of privacy, or debilitating conditions (nonsubtractive well-being) or to be independent of a sense of self-worth and the corresponding conditions of education and income (additive well-being) may pursue putative self-interests but compromise their genuine self-interest. Indeed, as I mentioned in passing, Gewirth includes among additive well-being certain "prudential virtues" (courage, temperance, prudence) which seem only to enrich the notion of genuine happiness.

But it must be remembered that these aspects of well-being are, by definition, *generic* capacities for action, capacities for being an agent who pursues particular purposes. In this respect, they do not differ in principle from Friedman's notion that genuine freedom implies the education requisite to being an informed person, or one who knows the relevant facts regarding his or her potential exchanges. It might be said that a distinction between putative and genuine self-interests is also included in Friedman's theory. Persons who will not acquire the requisite education or who take mind-stultifying drugs may pursue putative self-interest but compromise their genuine self-interest. But saying this does not alter the fact that Friedman's informed agents exercise their freedom in pursuit of wants that are solely a matter of preference; there is no ethical criterion in accord with which good wants may be defined. If we say that the condition of genuine freedom permits a notion of genuine self-interest, then, the term "self-interest" is used ambiguously. Persons who pursue particular preferences or wants and wish to continue doing so do indeed have an inescapable interest in the necessary conditions of doing so, such that action which destroys those conditions contradicts their intent to continue as free persons. But the self-interest which those conditions define is of a different order precisely because they are capacities required for the continuing pursuit of any particular preference or wants at all. It is, then, wants or self-interests in the particular sense which, for Friedman, are solely a matter of preference. Accordingly, it is among *these* that there is no distinction between putative and genuine ones.

Similarly, Gewirth's notion of well-being consists in the necessary conditions for being fully a prospective agent and, therefore, defines a self-interest which any prospective agent has. The complexity of generic goods notwithstanding, however, it does not follow that there is a criterion of genuine self-interest with respect to the particular purposes for which generic capacities are exercised. To be sure, the greater complexity in comparison to Friedman's informed and effectively free person places correspondingly greater constraints upon the things an agent may pursue consistent with being a prospective agent. Nonetheless, particular self-interest may still be solely a matter of preference in a way strictly analogous to Friedman's theory. It is these particular self-interests that I have in mind in saying that Gewirth's theory is an illustration of established liberalism.

But what reason is there to say that particular self-interests are, for Gewirth, solely matters of preference? Precisely the fact that the supreme normative principle prescribes *only* an equality of generic capacities for action. Prospective purposive agents are morally evaluated, in other words, only in those aspects whereby their actions affect the necessary conditions for any agent to act. There is no moral criterion by virtue of which the particular purposes or self-interests may be evaluated in those aspects whereby they do not affect generic goods. If "self-interest" refers to particular purposes in these latter aspects, moral claims in Gewirth's theory, as in Friedman's, refer solely to the proper relations between individuals of whose self-interests those claims are logically independent. In sum, the PGC does not *prescribe* particular purposes; it assumes that agents have chosen to pursue them.

It follows that Gewirth shares with Friedman what I have called the apparent "partialist fallacy," namely, that human activity may be morally good or right in part even though activities as wholes are nonmoral.

According to Gewirth, action may be moral in the respect that it affects the equal distribution of generic capacities, but the particular interests or purposes for whose realization these capacities are affirmed are solely a matter of preference. Given that action as a whole is defined by the purposes it seeks to realize, its effect upon the distribution of generic capacities is an abstract aspect of it. It is this restriction of moral reference to a part of action that accounts for the limitation upon the independent sector that I have discussed, namely, that associations are not included therein by virtue of their concrete religious, cultural, or educational purposes but in the abstract respect that those purposes are instrumental to generic rights.

But if these considerations confirm that Gewirth's theory includes the preferential view of particular interests, nothing which has been said shows that Gewirth's argument has failed. Even the "partialist fallacy" is, for all that I have said to this point, only apparent. Whatever force it may have rests on an appeal to intuition. Thus, Gewirth's argument from solely preferential agency to the PGC is implicitly an attempt to prove that the apparent "partialist fallacy" is in truth no fallacy at all, so that our intuitions, if they indeed make the fallacy apparent, are in this case misleading. On the other hand, if the preferential view of particular interests is false, then Gewirth's argument for the PGC must be unsuccessful. Of course, to show that his argument fails does not prove that partialism is a fallacy; some other argument for the preferential view of happiness may succeed. But the failure of Gewirth's argument is a necessary condition for the claim that established liberalism is wrong. Accordingly, I will now attempt to criticize Gewirth's defense of a supreme moral principle. I do so with more than the usual reservation required in philosophical argument. Gewirth's sophistication with respect to the relevant philosophical issues and resources, and the power and precision of his reasoning, are awesome. Given the respect which his achievement commands, one's initial suspicion is that seeming mistakes only appear because one has not thought as thoroughly as has he, and I have found this to be the case more than once. Still, I believe that the argument is not successful and that it fails precisely because it assumes particular purposes which are solely preferential in character.

The discussion will be served by a review of the steps in Gewirth's justification of the PGC.

(1) Because all practical precepts guide, advise, or urge people to fashion their behavior reflectively in accord with those precepts, action is generically voluntary and purposive.

(2) In voluntarily pursuing some purpose, the agent necessarily

claims that his or her purpose is at least prudentially good; "I do X for purpose E" entails "E is good," i.e., "E seems to me good."

(3) The agent necessarily claims that the generic features of his or her action are at least prudentially good.

(4) The agent necessarily claims at least prudential rights to generic freedom and well-being, in the sense that others ought not to interfere with these capacities.

(5) By the logical principle of universalizability, the agent necessarily claims the PGC.

Accepting (1), I should note that Gewirth's use of "good" in (2) does not contradict the claim that particular purposes are solely matters of preference. The agent's implied claim is not that he or she pursues E *because* E is good; rather, because he or she pursues E, this purpose "seems to me good." Gewirth insists that "good" is here used in a "broad sense encompassing a wide range of non-moral as well as moral criteria" (49), and the agent is only committed to the claim that E is *at least prudentially* good. Thus, "E is good" is another way of expressing the fact that X is chosen by a rational agent, such that this choice has prescriptive force for the agent with respect to other choices which prudential rationality then requires. If this meaning is maintained, everything which follows from "E is good" will also follow from "I choose to pursue E" or "I want E, at least inclinationally." Since I have used the phrase "solely a matter of preference" to designate human purposes or choices for which there is putatively no moral criterion, the reasoning might also proceed from "I (solely) prefer E." Accordingly, we may say that Gewirth's argument seeks to show what an agent necessarily prefers as a consequence of any particular preference at all. In (3), for instance, Gewirth argues that any particular preference entails a preference for one's own generic freedom and well-being, just because these capacities are necessary means or conditions for agency. It would be self-contradictory for an agent to say that he or she prefers to pursue E but does not prefer the necessary conditions for achieving that end.

Referring to (4), Gewirth himself speaks of "the crucial importance of this thesis for my overall argument" (63). As he probably expected, most critics of his theory have focused upon the rights-claim, contending that it does not follow from (3). I cite E. M. Adams to illustrate this critique:

> Perhaps we can . . . grant Gewirth's claim that if one recognizes that Y is a necessary condition for his attainment of any X that he may desire, he must, on pain of inconsistency, regard Y as a

> necessary (unconditional, indispensable) good. These inferences would be based on the connection between what one regards as good and what he desires. This connection, however, is not enough for the next step in Gewirth's argument. It does not, insofar as I can see, warrant the conclusion that, if one regards his own freedom and well-being as necessary goods, he must, on pain of inconsistency, regard them as rights, which entail obligations on the part of others. All the connection between "good" and desire would seem to warrant at this point would be that the agent, with his judgment that his freedom and well-being are indispensable goods, would, on pain of inconsistency, desire and even regard as an indispensable good, that others not interfere with his freedom and well being" (E. M. Adams, 585; for alternative statements of the same critique, see Veatch, 410 and MacIntyre, 64–65).

In other words, Adams concedes (3) and, therefore, correctly concedes, "The agent necessarily claims that non-interference with his or her freedom and well-being is good"; but Adams denies that the agent must hold that others are *obligated* not to interfere, i.e., denies that a rights-claim is entailed by (3). Given the concession, however, I am prepared to defend Gewirth's argument. It may be reviewed in the following way: Assume any agent, A, who necessarily claims that A's freedom and well-being and, therefore, noninterference by others with these generic capacities are good. Now presume that A cannot be certain that B, any other agent, will not be successful should B try to interfere with A's freedom and well-being. It follows that A necessarily holds, "It is bad for B to try to interfere with A's generic capacities." But A is then committed to the claim, "It is bad that B is, qua agent, rationally permitted to try to interfere with A's generic capacities"; for, if B is so permitted, B should attempt this interference whenever, by prudential reasoning, B's particular purposes so require. Thus, A must claim, "It is good that B is, qua agent, rationally required to refrain from interference with A's freedom and well-being." But this last claim implies a rights-claim; if B is rationally required qua agent to refrain from interference with A, then B is duty-bound to do so, and this duty implies A's rights to freedom and well-being. Summarily stated, A's claim that his or her agency is necessarily good implies the claim that others are morally bound to refrain from interference. But A's rights-claim is prudential in character, because it states a necessary condition for any of A's prudential purposes. Thus, Adams cannot concede (3) and consistently deny (4).

Adams might respond that A's rights-claim cannot be necessary unless B is in truth rationally required qua agent in the manner specified.

A's agency cannot commit him or her to a claim specifying B's moral obligation if it is not true that B has that obligation. Thus, Adams might continue, Gewirth's derivation of A's rights-claim implies a moral principle which binds the agency of B, and this implication is illicit because that moral principle has not been justified (Adams seems to suggest this response; see 586). Gewirth, of course, would not deny that the derivation of (4) from (3) implies a moral principle; indeed, were this not so, he could not hold that (4) implies the PGC. But he would deny, and I think rightly, that the implication is illicit. If (3) is true, then, as we have just seen, the agency of A entails A's rights-claim; accordingly, B would not be morally bound in the manner specified only if A were not an agent. The conclusion remains that Adams's concession and his denial are contradictory, and that Gewirth's derivation of (4) from (3) is valid. The logical principle of universalizability then makes explicit what is implicit in (4), namely, that A necessarily claims, "It is good that A is qua agent rationally required not to interfere with the freedom and well-being of B." Agency as such, Gewirth concludes, commits one to the PGC, so that one may rationally avoid its requirement only by "disavowing and refraining from . . . the whole sphere of practice" (29).

Notwithstanding that the criticism by Adams misses the mark, I do not think that Gewirth's project is successful. Its failure, I will now argue, follows from the seemingly harmless proviso that one might avoid the PGC by disavowing and refraining from the whole sphere of practice. Another way to express this proviso is to say that the PGC does not require a person to be an agent. On the contrary, one is bound by the PGC only *if*, as Gewirth puts it, one chooses "to move from quiescence or non-action to action" (49). One might think that this qualification is only a tongue-in-cheek manner of saying that there is no way to escape the PGC, because it is impossible for a person in the present not to choose and, therefore, not to act. Even the decision to make one's present action one's last is a choice or an action. But the proviso is substantive, precisely because one *can* choose to disavow *future* action or, in Gewirth's term, choose whether or not to be a "prospective agent." It is only in the sense that one genuinely chooses to be an agent that one's purposes "seem to him to be good" (49), so that Gewirth's argument for the PGC may begin. If, to the contrary, one necessarily is or will be an agent, action may be simply an arbitrary choice where some practice cannot be avoided, and action is not, therefore, necessarily conative in Gewirth's sense. Thus, Gewirth writes that the agent regards his or her goal "as worth aiming at or pursuing; for if he did not so regard it he would not unforcedly choose to move from quiescence or nonaction to action with a view to achieving the goal" (49). "Even in the case of arbitrarily chosen actions he at least wants to perform some action rather than none" (51). Gewirth cannot hold that one endorses one's own agency, that one claims rights to freedom and well-being, unless one genuinely chooses one's own agency. Accordingly, one can escape the requirements of the PGC if one chooses not to be a prospective agent.

I will call the choice of whether or not to be a prospective agent a person's "constitutive choice," and in this way express its distinction from the choices between particular purposes which agency itself implies. The distinction may be formulated as follows: a person's constitutive choice is whether or not to have particular purposes (whether or not to be a prospective agent); an agent's choice (which presupposes a constitutive choice to be a prospective agent) is between possible particular purposes. To be sure, one cannot choose to be a prospective agent without also choosing, or at least intending to choose, some particular future purpose or purposes. But that implication does not erase the distinction between choosing to be a future actor and choosing among the possible actions which future agency permits, precisely because the latter presupposes that one has not chosen to refrain from the whole sphere of practice. Just because Gewirth's argument for the PGC also presupposes that a person has chosen to be a prospective agent, the constitutive choice itself cannot be morally required. A person's constitutive choice is itself solely a matter of preference.

I will now contend that there is a suppressed and, in Gewirth's own terms, contradictory premise in his argument to the effect that solely preferential constitutive choices must be unqualified. Gewirth implicitly asserts that one must choose to be a prospective agent without qualification *or* to disavow agency without qualification. I will attempt presently to show why this suppressed premise is both required by Gewirth's project and contradictory in his own terms. But attention should first be directed to what the premise means.

Formally, a third alternative seems possible for a person's constitutive choice, namely, the choice to be a prospective agent with qualification and, therefore, also to disavow agency with qualification. Given that the choice is solely a matter of preference, there is no reason, at least to first appearances, why a person should not choose in this way. Gewirth, of course, may respond that the putative third alternative makes no sense and, therefore, is in truth impossible. To the contrary, the possibility is confirmed by the fact that people do choose it. Consider a person who prefers or chooses an overriding commitment to the realization of some state of affairs which he or she takes to be ideal, for instance, a utopian society or the reign of God's will on earth. If this choice is one's constitutive choice, or informs it, one will necessarily choose to be a prospective agent insofar as one's agency might contribute to or be required by the ideal-to-be-realized. By parity of reasoning, however, one's choice to be a prospective agent will be made with the qualification that one's agency is at least consistent with that ideal. This constitutive choice may be formulated as follows: I choose to be a prospective agent unless a situation arises in which the ideal-to-be-realized is best served at the expense of my agency, at the extreme by my death, in which case I choose to disavow and refrain from the field of practice insofar as the ideal requires. I emphasize that this qualification is a part of one's present constitutive choice, because one's preference for the overriding ideal is one's choice to be a prospective agent, or informs that choice. Thus, one also chooses now that one's freedom and well-being should be interfered with insofar as one does at any time mistakenly believe that they are consistent with the ideal-to-be-realized. Although questions may be raised regarding who will be assigned responsibility for making this judgment, these do not affect the substantive point: if in truth one's future freedom and well-being compromise the ideal-to-be-realized, and if at that time one should deny this truth, one now chooses that one's agency should be interfered with in service to the ideal.

In saying that Gewirth's argument presupposes constitutive choices without qualification, I mean that the suppressed premise rules out such qualified choices as I have just illustrated. If this illustration confirms the possibility of such qualified choices, it also shows by implication why they are problematic for Gewirth's theory. Given that one chooses to be a prospective agent with the qualification of an ideal-to-be-realized, one will be committed to the following claim: "It is good for me to try to interfere with the freedom and well-being of others insofar as such interference is required by the ideal." To be sure, by the logical principle of universalizability, this agent must also claim: "It is good for my freedom and well-being to be interfered with insofar as such interference is required by the ideal." But, as we have just seen, this claim is no longer inconsistent with the constitutive choice to be a prospective agent, since that choice was made with precisely this qualification. This agent, then, will not be committed, upon pain of inconsistency, to the PGC, and, accordingly, Gewirth's argument depends upon the suppressed premise that such agency is impossible.

Characteristically, Gewirth anticipates something like this criticism and discusses the person I have described in his explication of the rights-claim. A "fanatic," he says, is "a person who agrees to the overriding of his own self-interest when this conflicts with some ideal he sincerely upholds'' (96), but Gewirth argues that the fanatic presents no problem to his thesis: ''So long as . . . the fanatic is prepared to act in support of his ideal, he has purposes he wants to fulfill. Hence, he must, if he is rational, hold that he has generic rights required for his purpose-fulfilling actions, even if the purposes in question are ultimately designed to prevent his continuing to be an agent'' (96). But this response, I think, misses the point. If the fanatic's overriding ideal is or informs the constitutive choice to be a prospective agent, then this person is ''prepared to act'' or ''has purposes he wants to fulfill'' only insofar as his or her agency is consistent with that ideal. Thus, the endorsement of his or her own freedom and well-being is similarly qualified, so that he or she is not committed to the rights-claim upon which Gewirth insists. Gewirth, in other words, presupposes precisely what is being questioned, namely, that this person chooses to be a prospective agent without qualification and then chooses the overriding ideal as one of alternative possible purposes. Were that the case, the ideal would not in truth be overriding, since the fanatic would be committed to disavowing the ideal should it come in conflict with his or her agency and would not really be a fanatic.

In further comments upon the fanatic, Gewirth argues that an overriding ideal must be held as a normative or rationally justifiable principle and is, therefore, illicitly introduced into the argument. ''In holding that if he had certain qualities he would no longer have rights to freedom and well-being, the fanatic is giving priority to a specific normative criterion for having such rights'' (96). But I see no reason why a fanatic must hold that his or her overriding ideal is rationally justifiable. On the contrary, given that the constitutive choice is solely a matter of preference, the fanatic is free to qualify his or her choice as he or she pleases. If, however, Gewirth means that the ideal must be rationally justifiable in order properly to hold that it overrides one's rights to freedom and well-being, then the question at issue has been begged. For the point is that the fanatic's constitutive choice to be a prospective agent does not imply the generic rights-claim. Thus, when Gewirth goes on to conclude that this normative principle is illicitly introduced into the sequence of reasoning because only a principle derived from the concept of action is rationally justifiable, the question is also begged. For *whether* a supreme moral principle can be derived from Gewirth's concept of action is precisely the point at issue. In other words, Gewirth here again stipulates by implication that one's constitutive choice must be made without qualification in order that a supreme moral principle might be derived. That this stipulation is gratuitous, so that no moral principle follows from Gewirth's concept of action, is precisely what the possibility of fanatics is designed to show.

If the fanatic avoids a commitment to the PGC, escape is also available without a constitutive commitment to an overriding ideal. A person might choose to be a prospective agent with the following qualification: so long as or insofar as I can prevent others who so try from interfering with my freedom and well-being. Such an agent would not be committed in any respect to the claim that others ought not to interfere with his or her freedom and well-being; this person endorses his or her own generic capacities only insofar as he or she can prevent that interference when it is attempted and, therefore, chooses not to be an agent insofar as others succeed in that attempt. Given this qualification, there is in no respect an implied endorsement of the agency of others. This person is rationally free to try to interfere with others whenever his or her particular purposes require. To be sure, one must have some particular purposes for the sake of which one tries to interfere with others and to prevent their interference with oneself. Given that the constitutive choice is solely a matter of preference, however, there is no reason why having these particular purposes cannot be qualified in the manner specified. With such a qualification, a person is, we might say, prepared to live in a Hobbesian state of nature, so that we may call this the Hobbesian qualification.

But now, if *any* person *may* choose prospective agency with the Hobbesian qualification, it then follows that *all* persons who choose prospective agency *must* do so with this qualification. For if anyone is rationally permitted to try to interfere with others as he or she pleases, there can be no supreme moral principle, so that no agent is morally required to respect the interests or purposes of others in any respect. Accordingly, each person who chooses to be a prospective agent necessarily accepts a world of human interaction that is thoroughly nonmoral in character. But this means that Gewirth's suppressed premise is, given his understanding of agency, contradictory. If all constitutive choices are solely matters of preference, then *no* choice to be a prospective agent can be without qualification; every prospective agent chooses to be so with the Hobbesian qualification.

It is now clear where Adams's critique goes amiss. In conceding (3), he implicitly accepts the suppressed premise that prospective agents must choose to be so without qualification. As he recognizes, he must then accept, "An agent necessarily claims that non-interference with his or her generic capacities is good," and, as I have discussed, Adams cannot consistently deny (4). Given that constitutive choices are solely a matter of preference, however, the premise cannot be true; prospective agents necessarily choose to be so with the Hobbesian qualification. Thus, one should not concede (3). An agent does not necessarily claim that his or her agency as such is good; rather, an agent necessarily claims that his or her agency as such is good insofar as he or she can prevent others who so try from interfering. It then follows that agency also does not imply that noninterference with the agent's freedom and well-being is good; rather, an agent necessarily claims something like, "It is good that others who so prefer try to interfere with my freedom and well-being." Accordingly, (4) is not true. Of course, if one should not concede (3), neither should one concede (2), for (2) implies (3). An agent does not necessarily claim that his or her purpose is good; this could be true only if the constitutive choice must be made without qualification. An agent necessarily claims that his or her particular purpose is good insofar as he or she can prevent others who so try from interfering with its realization. It may seem strange for an agent to accept the Hobbesian qualification and thereby implicitly claim, "It is good for others who so prefer to try to interfere with my agency." But the point is that this claim is the price of choosing to be an agent when that choice is solely a matter of preference. The war of each against all may not be a pleasant world to enter; but, if one thinks so, one should choose to disavow and refrain from the whole sphere of practice.

If this line of internal criticism has merit, it shows that Gewirth has failed to justify the PGC. Given the solely preferential character of the constitutive choice, the nature of one's agency does not commit one to any moral principle at all. It commits prospective agents to the war of each against all. "Fanatics" may, if they wish, add whatever other qualifications they please to their agency within this world, but none can avoid the fact that "all is permitted." The point, finally, is that action which is inherently nonmoral cannot itself imply a moral principle, and for this reason Gewirth's argument cannot succeed without the suppressed premise that I have described. For, in truth, prospective agents *must* choose to be such without qualification only if human agency as such is morally required; given that prospective agency is itself a choice, one must *choose* agency in a certain way only if one *ought* to be an agent of that kind. But, then, the constitutive choice is not solely a matter of preference, and one cannot avoid moral requirements by choosing to disavow and refrain from the whole sphere of practice. Of course, Gewirth cannot say that the choice to be an agent is morally required, because his project would then presuppose rather than derive a moral principle. Accordingly, the premise is contradictory within his enterprise—and suppressed. Alternatively, we may say that Gewirth's moral theory is incoherent. The claim that prospective agency is solely a matter of preference is inconsistent with the assertion that human action is morally bound by the PGC.

As should be apparent by this point, I hold that the problem in Gewirth's project rests not in some illicit move within the argument but in the concept of action with which the argument begins. Intent upon deriving a supreme moral principle from the nature of agency, he simply assumes the choice to be an agent and thereby avoids the question of why action takes place at all, why people who could choose otherwise do choose to be prospective agents. It then follows that this constitutive choice must be solely preferential. It is worth noting that nothing which Gewirth says about practical precepts requires that the choice to be an agent have this character. Recall (1) "Because all practical precepts guide, advise, or urge people to fashion their behavior reflectively in accord with those precepts, action is generically voluntary and purposive." This, I think, is correct. But it does not imply that voluntariness and purposiveness are themselves chosen solely as a matter of preference. For all that has been said, human action may be morally bound to a comprehensive principle of choice in accord with which the constitutive choice to be a prospective agent is itself morally evaluated. Indeed, this is what I will argue in the chapters which follow.

In any event, Gewirth's claim that the constitutive choice has no moral criterion introduces the established liberal theory of happiness into his political theory. If this choice is solely preferential, so too are the agent's particular wants or purposes. Were a person morally bound to act, the particular purposes without which there can be no agency would also be morally required. The PGC, then, morally evaluates action only in the respect that the agent affects the distribution of generic opportunity to pursue solely preferential interests. Thus, if incoherence characterizes Gewirth's theory by virtue of his concept of action, it is also true that this failure is directly related to his affirmation of the preferential view of self-interest. Finally, it is this concept of action which makes Gewirth's theory an example of the apparent "partialist fallacy": action may be moral in an abstract aspect but is nonmoral as a whole. If I have not yet shown that this claim—and, therefore, the established liberal view of happiness—is always fallacious, I have tried to show that Gewirth does not prove it to be true.

Four

A Formal Condition for Political Theory

I have now reviewed two established liberal theories of human associations and, in each instance, developed the implied understanding of independent associations. This exercise alone displays the importance of political theory to the discussion of independent associations, because these two theoretical perspectives, notwithstanding that they fall within the same broad political tradition, lead to significant differences in the definition of the independent sector. Those differences may now be summarized.

In the theory of Milton Friedman, independent associations are defined as private and nonprofit and include both charitable institutions and nongovernmental associations formed for purposes of democratic political participation. This class properly excludes many organizations commonly included within the "third sector," e.g., most cultural associations, many religious communities, institutions of higher education, and most health-delivery organizations. These exclusions follow because independent associations, as governmental ones, are properly subservient in the social order to the profit-seeking sector and are justified only insofar as they serve or do not compromise maximal competitive capitalism. Private, nonprofit associations as such are theoretically significant because the same is true of profit-seeking institutions—the moral significance of the negative term, "nonprofit," is derivative from the corresponding positive, "profit-seeking." If an argument could be successfully advanced to the effect that profit-seeking institutions as such are only significant theoretically when, as with Friedman, they are to be maximized, it would follow that the common definition of the "third sector" is committed to something like nineteenth-century liberalism.

In the theory of Alan Gewirth, independent associations are defined as other-regarding associations, those in which people seek to be instrumental to the generic goods (freedom and well-being) of recipients, and this purpose may be pursued either directly (privately other-regarding associations) or through participation in the constitutional decision-procedures of the state (publicly other-regarding associations). This class is not co-extensive with nonprofit organizations as such, although all associations within it are nonprofit. Still, this class is more extensive than Friedman's independent sector, because it includes many cultural, religious, higher educational, and health-delivery, as well as many social-service, organizations. Strictly speaking, however, these organizations are part of the independent sector only insofar as they are instrumental to generic goods. Gewirth's independent sector is both a subclass of nonprofit organizations *and* more extensive than Friedman's, because nonprofit associations are not, in Gewirth's theory, subservient to profit-seeking ones. Indeed, for Gewirth, the distinction between profit-seeking and nonprofit is not theoretically significant.

It might be said that the common contemporary understanding of the "third sector" is informed, in some respects, by a muddled mixture of something like these two theories. With Friedman (and, insofar as he is representative, with nineteenth-century liberalism) it defines the sector as coextensive with private, nonprofit organizations; with Gewirth (and, insofar as he is representative, with twentieth-century liberalism) it includes within this sector cultural, religious, educational, and health-delivery institutions. In the absence of some alternative theory, in other words, the common view appears to consider "nonprofit" a significant theoretical term, even though it does not attribute significance to "profit-seeking" as such. To conclude that the common view is a theoretical muddle would help explain why, as I noted at the outset of this work, there is precious little clarity in current discussion regarding the nature and importance of independent associations.

In any event, what Friedman and Gewirth have in common, I have argued, is established liberalism's preferential view of happiness or self-interest. As a consequence, they share the implication that independent associations, like all others, are morally significant because they serve in some specified way solely preferential self-interests. I have tried to show that a fundamental incoherence in each of the two theories is directly related to just this liberal view of happiness. That conclusion at least raises the question of whether any theory inclusive of this view must also be similarly problematic, i.e., whether established liberalism as such fails to provide a convincing understanding of our associational life. I have implied that this is so by suggesting that these two theories are instances of a general "partialist fallacy" by which established liberalism as such is characterized. But the grounds for calling this a fallacy have been intuitive. In contrast, the present chapter will seek to show that partialism is indeed fallacious and thereby will seek to invalidate the preferential view of self-interest as such. This conclusion will be contained within a more inclusive constructive argument regarding moral evaluation. The argument seeks to defend a formal condition for political theory, namely, that an acceptable political theory must be informed by a comprehensive moral principle. The purpose of this chapter, then, is not only to move beyond established liberalism but also to set the formal terms within which other theories of associations might be assessed.

An Argument Proposed

The argument will proceed through an appropriation of Gewirth's "dialectically necessary method," at least in the following respect: I intend to show that human activity entails a moral principle in accord with which human choice as such may be evaluated. "Human choice as such" refers to the alternatives for all human choices in all aspects, or all human activities as wholes. The formal condition for political theory is that such theory must be informed by a moral principle which evaluates human activity comprehensively. If this is so, the established liberal view of happiness is invalid. As stated in chapter 1 and illustrated with reference to Friedman and Gewirth, the view that happiness is solely preferential implies that moral claims refer solely to the proper relations between various individuals of whose self-interests those claims are logically independent. Both Friedman and Gewirth prescribe the equal distribution of general capacities for the pursuit of preferences (equal opportunity for happiness), and this similarity is not compromised by the fact that these capacities are relatively simple in Friedman (freedom) and relatively complex in Gewirth (freedom and well-being). Just because moral evaluation is logically independent of self-interests, there is no comprehensive moral principle. This is, of course, another way to say that established liberal theories are partialist in the sense that I have called fallacious. Because self-interest is solely a matter of preference, some aspects of human activities (and, therefore, human activities as wholes) cannot be morally evaluated. Success in defending comprehensive moral evaluation as a formal condition for political theory will confirm that partialism is a fallacy and invalidate the preferential view of happiness as such.

Before I proceed with the argument, a clarification of the term "moral evaluation" is in order. For Gewirth, as we have seen, morality involves "a set of categorically obligatory requirements for action" (Gewirth, 1). Similarly, I will use "moral evaluation" to mean a comparison of alternatives for human choice in which the categorically required choice or class of choices is directly or indirectly identified. In so putting the matter, I intend to restrict moral evaluations to what are sometimes called *substantive* moral evaluations, evaluations which distinguish between real choice-alternatives or classes thereof. In contrast, some have held that moral evaluations may be purely formal in character. It has been said, for instance, that agents are morally bound to universalize their judgments, although the substance or content to be universalized is not morally prescribed (see Hare 1961; 1965). Whether or not such an evaluation is purely formal need not be debated here (elsewhere, I have tried to show that it is not (see Gamwell, 44–48). My purpose is rather so to define moral evaluations that they are implicitly or explicitly substantive in character.

An alternative is categorically required when it is required independently of any condition that is simultaneously chosen by the human in question. Categorical requirements are objective requirements and are distinguished from hypothetical ones, the latter referring to choices that are required *if* the human in question simultaneously chooses some specified condition. If a person chooses to pursue a larger income, he or she may be required to work overtime, but the requirement is hypothetical because it is dependent upon a condition which is simultaneously chosen by the human in question. The moment this person chooses not to pursue a higher income, the requirement vanishes. In contrast, the statement "A ought to tell the truth" (or, "telling the truth is for A the morally good or right choice") represents a moral claim when it means that some choice which does not constitute lying is for A required independently of any condition which is simultaneously open to A's choice. The categorical requirement may be dependent upon a prior choice by the person in question; for instance, A may be morally bound to do a certain thing for B by virtue of A's prior choice to promise such action. This emphasizes that the distinction between categorical and hypothetical requirements rests upon conditions that are *simultaneously* chosen by the agent. In this sense, only moral evaluation constitutes a reason for choice that is independent of the choice; or, alternatively, all such reasons are moral ones.

It is true that many evaluations generally said to be moral ones are not so formulated as to identify directly categorically required choices. Such formulations may, for instance, refer directly to choices that are morally proscribed or morally permitted. But evaluations formulated in either of these ways identify categorically required choices indirectly and may be reformulated without loss of moral meaning to do so directly. The statement "X is a morally proscribed choice" may be reformulated, "Some choice other than X is categorically required." "A ought not to lie" is equivalent to "some choice other than lying is for A categorically required." Similarly, the statement "X is a morally permissible choice" may be reformulated, "No choice other than X is categorically required." Although I will not pursue the matter here, extended discussion would, in my judgment, confirm that all other explicit moral evaluations (e.g., regarding moral culpability, moral virtue or character, moral associations) may be reformulated to identify directly categorically required human choices. In any event, I mean to include all statements which can be so reformulated when I say that a moral evaluation is a comparison of alternatives for human choice in which the categorically required choice or class of choices is *directly or indirectly* identified. It is a comprehensive principle for evaluation in this sense that, I will now argue, is entailed by human activity.

Self-Conscious Activity

It will be recalled that Gewirth discovers the generic features of action by examining what the objects of all practical precepts have in common. Because all such precepts "guide, advise, or urge" (Gewirth, 26) people to fashion their behavior reflectively in accord with those precepts, he concludes that action is generically voluntary and purposive. But it also follows that human action is generically self-conscious, that agents can know or understand what they are doing. Were this not so, they could not fashion their behavior reflectively. It might well be argued that individuals to whom we refer as humans are not always self-conscious (e.g., they sleep) and, moreover, that self-consciousness itself is a matter of more or less, so that creatures which we do not call humans may be self-conscious in some measure. Nonetheless, it can be agreed that a significant measure of self-consciousness is the characteristic of *distinctively* human activity. Accordingly, any creature or individual who has the capacity for significant self-consciousness (whether presently exercised or not) is appropriately called human, and it is such self-consciousness which is implied by all practical precepts.

In distinctively human activity, then, one exercises a capacity to understand oneself and, thereby, the world to which one is related. To be sure, "understanding" is itself a difficult thing to understand with precision, and the pursuit of an understanding of understanding is both fascinating and important. For present purposes, however, that issue need not detain us. It is sufficient to direct our attention to the experience of self-consciousness (which is presupposed in the attempt to understand understanding) and to the necessary assumption that this consciousness can be in varying measure correct or true. The capacity to understand oneself is, in other words, the capacity to know oneself. Absent that assumption, all inquiry and conversation ceases. The present argument seeks to derive a formal condition for moral theory that is implied by distinctively human activity.

The self-understanding characteristic of human activity is not necessarily reflective, where "reflective" means that a self-understanding is more or less thematized or conceptualized. It is true, as Gewirth says, that all practical precepts assume the ability to reflect upon action, but he also agrees that behavior may be voluntary and purposive without this ability being fully engaged (see, e.g., Gewirth, 38). In any event, the human capacity is not only to know or understand oneself but also to know or understand that one knows or understands oneself. Thus, reflective self-consciousness is the attempt to express thematically or conceptually a primordial or immediate self-understanding that logically precedes it and that is, perhaps, better connoted by the term "self-awareness." When self-consciousness is said to mean the reflective experience, the level of self-awareness seems to be "preconscious." In truth, however, the latter may be understood as a kind of self-understanding (see Ogden, 1971).

It is also apparent that one can misunderstand oneself, that one's self-understanding, at either immediate or reflective levels, may be in some measure false. Nonetheless, self-consciousness also implies the possibility of correct self-understanding (or, alternatively, the *capacity* to know oneself). For this reason, we might say that a false understanding is always in some measure "self-deception." In other words, the term "self-understanding" is systematically ambiguous. On the one hand, it denotes any understanding of the self, correct or not; on the other hand, it denotes the correct self-understanding which any self-understanding implies and purports to be. It is worth noting that precisely this human capacity for self-consciousness makes possible the attempt to formulate theories of human action. Whatever else it is, one's own action is an instance of human action generally. Consequently, self-understanding always includes an understanding of the nature of human action, and the pursuit of a theory of action is the attempt to bring this understanding to fully reflective expression. In other words, a theory of human action is always a generalized self-understanding.

Self-consciousness implies the freedom which Gewirth takes to be generic to human action. Self-conscious activity is, as I prefer to say, in part self-determined, where the contrary of self-determination is other-determination, and the denial that human activity is in part self-determined is the assertion that the activity is completely the effect of causes other than itself. Further, self-determination means an "unforced choice," a choice among genuine alternatives. To say that there is only one alternative for the self to "choose" is identical to the claim that the self is completely determined by others. Self-consciousness implies genuine choice because, whatever others are causes of the activity, these others cannot also cause a consciousness or understanding of their effects. Let any others determine the activity in any way you please, self-consciousness means an understanding of precisely *these* determinations; thus, the understanding cannot be one of the determinations in question. Alternatively stated, self-consciousness permits the self to say "I," to distinguish between itself and the others that have an effect upon it, and this distinction cannot itself be the effect of another. Self-consciousness is in some way transcendent to, not exhausted by, other-determination; it is in some way an expression of self-determination, of a choice from among alternatives.

It should be emphasized that this conclusion does not imply a complete indeterminism with respect to human activity, such that activity fully constitutes itself. Self-consciousness entails determination by others in some measure just as it also implies self-determination. Were the former absent, there would not be anything of which the self could be conscious. In understanding itself, human activity simultaneously understands the world of which it is an effect, i.e., it is conscious of being constituted in part by that world. Other-determination, then, limits the alternatives among which human activity may choose. The point is that other-determination cannot eliminate those alternatives. Nothing has been said here to resolve debates regarding the ways in which humans are limited by their circumstances, except insofar as such resolution is implied by human self-consciousness as such. If activity is human, it must also be in some measure a matter of choice, and any measure of self-conscious choice at all will suffice for the present argument.

We are now in a position to see why one's self-understanding may be in some measure false. The choice involved in human activity is, or at least includes, a choice among self-understandings. Choosing to constitute oneself according to one alternative is to understand oneself and the world to which one is related differently than if another alternative were chosen. This is all the more important if, as the argument in this chapter seeks to show, every self-understanding implies a comprehensive moral principle according to which alternatives for choice are compared and evaluated. Given that conclusion, one's choice always implies an understanding of this comprehensive principle and, therefore, of good and bad (or right and wrong) activity. The choice of an alternative that is in truth morally prohibited is at some level of understanding the affirmation of a false moral principle; it is, or includes, the choice of a false self-understanding. To note that self-deception is involved in false self-understanding is another way of saying that the self chooses a more or less false self-understanding when a correct understanding was an alternative.

The Comprehensive Moral Principle

Self-conscious choice, I will now argue, implies a comprehensive moral principle. The argument will proceed in two principal steps, showing (1) that any correct self-understanding requires a comprehensive variable in accord with which human choice as such may be correctly understood, and (2) that this comprehensive variable must be morally evaluative. The second step will have two subsections, showing (i) that no categorically required choice can be correctly understood or identified without a comparison of human choice as such, and (ii) that there must be categorically required choices. If some choices are categorically required and their identification requires a comparison of human choice as such, it will follow that the comparative variable in terms of which human choice as such is correctly understood is a comprehensive moral principle.

Understanding

Were it the case that a given human activity is completely determined by others, knowing the situation in which this activity occurs would be sufficient to know what the activity is, since the activity would be totally a product of the situation. If Robert Frost, arriving where two roads diverged in a yellow wood, were determined by others to take the one less traveled by, then a correct understanding of his arrival would imply this action. Because self-conscious activity is in part self-determined, however, it is not only a product of its situation but also a choice between alternatives that the situation leaves open—the situation, let us say, plus the choice of X rather than Y. Human activity is something that could have been different, and that it could have been Y is part of what the *choice* of X is. Frost cannot correctly understand himself without knowing that he could have chosen the well-worn path. In sum, unless human activity is understood as X rather than Y, it is not understood as the consequence of choice.

But correctly understanding X rather than Y involves comparing the alternatives; the similarities and differences between them must be understood if the understanding of choice is to have any specific content. In turn, comparison necessarily involves a variable in terms of which the similarities and differences are specified, a variable of which the alternatives are instances in similar or differing ways. The variable, it should be emphasized, is one of which both X and Y are instances, for only so can the comparison be positive or determinate. It will not do to say that one choice is a path less trod while the other is not. In such a statement, the action is understood as a choice of X rather than not-X, where not-X could be anything other than a path less trod. Indeed, strictly speaking, not-X refers to nothing at all, so that designating an activity as X rather than as not-X does not even identify the reality of an alternative. In truth, however, the activity is a choice of X rather than Y, of the less trod rather than the well-worn path. In order correctly to understand the action, then, there must be a variable (for instance, extent of previous travel) of which both alternatives can be determinate or positive instances.

I now wish to argue that the variable according to which alternatives for a particular activity are correctly understood always implies a comprehensive variable for comparing choice alternatives as such, a variable that is objective and one in terms of which all choice alternatives may be compared in all aspects. The understanding of a particular activity always implies a variable which, were it made fully reflective, would define a theory of human activity. All theories of human activity are implicitly or explicitly based upon some comprehensive comparative variable, such that any human activity is understood as a specific instance or example of the variable, and its distinction from all other activities is understandable in terms provided by the variable. The kind of variable I intend here is exemplified by the place of pleasure in the psychology of some hedonists: all choices are properly compared in terms of the pleasure of the agent. Some economists have compared all choice alternatives with respect to their exchange value in a competitive market; some sociologists hold that the proper comparison of choices is the extent to which alternatives contribute to the equilibrium or stability of the social system.

I return to a particular human activity and the alternatives involved. Even if the variable through which that activity is correctly understood is not comprehensive, still this variable cannot itself be a matter of choice. Were that the case, there would be no correct understanding, since the understanding waits upon the variable chosen. The understanding that follows from being a hedonist, for instance, would be correct if one chose to be a hedonist, but incorrect if one did not. Thus, the comparative variable for correct understanding of a human action must be *objective*, i.e., independent of the agent's choice.

Again, it cannot be the case that some human activities are correctly understood in terms of one objective variable and others in terms of another, such that there is no single variable for comparing all choice alternatives. A claim to this effect would assert a kind of relativism in human understanding, according to which all variables for understanding human activity are relative to more or less specific human conditions. In taking issue with such relativism, I do not mean to deny that choice alternatives may be similar or different in a vast number of more or less specific ways. Difference in terms of the extent of previous travel is a specific difference and compares only certain choices, e.g., those in which one chooses between paths. Similarly, difference in terms of the peculiar characteristics of American culture or "the modern condition" is still a specific difference and relative to certain choices, those taken by people who are affected by that culture or that condition. It is precisely the increased appreciation of such specific differences which has made cognitive or epistemological relativism in some form or another widely attractive in modern thought. But there is no escaping the fact that all truth cannot be relative, because the assertion that it is so is clearly nonrelative in character. Similarly, to say that different situations of choice are correctly understood through different objective variables is to make a nonrelative assertion about the correct understanding of human choice; in other words, relativism is a nonrelative theory and, therefore, self-refuting. In order to understand that there are specifically different conditions of human choice (specific differences of culture, historical age, etc.), one must have an understanding of those differences and, therefore, a comparative variable that is nonrelative. The specific variables relative to specific conditions must themselves be specifications of, because comparable by, a nonspecific variable that is *supreme*, a variable in terms of which all human choices are properly understood.

Finally, the supreme comparative variable must compare all choice alternatives in all aspects, because it is the variable through which all human choice alternatives can be correctly understood. One might suggest that some aspects of at least some choices cannot be understood. But I hold that this suggestion is, like epistemological relativism, self-refuting. One could not know that this state of affairs is so much as a possibility without understanding the aspects which, it is said, might be beyond understanding. Merely knowing what is suggested presupposes what the suggestion denies. "The unknowable," as Whitehead succinctly puts the matter, "is unknown" (1929, 6). One may also say that the supreme variable must compare all conceivable aspects of human choices, since conceivable aspects are understandable. Inconceivable aspects are, of course, inconceivable. Thus, the supreme variable in question is *comprehensive*, it compares human choice as such.

Moral Evaluation

If human activity entails a comprehensive variable in terms of which human choice as such is correctly understood, it also implies a comprehensive moral principle, on condition only that the variable in question is morally evaluative. Of course, a considerable tradition in modern human science denies just this condition. Sometimes purporting to derive from Max Weber or David Hume or both, perspectives within this tradition hold that theories of human activity should be (or at least can be) "value-free," in the sense that a correct understanding of human activity is logically independent of all, and therefore does not require any, moral affirmations or commitments (see, e.g., Easton 1953, 219–32; 1965, 1–22). Given that such an understanding does require a comprehensive variable for comparing choice alternatives, this "value-free" claim can be true *only if* one of the two following claims is also true: (i) Although assertions of the form "X is a categorically required choice" are meaningful, i.e., may be true, the identification of these choices does not require a comparison of human choice as such. (ii) Putative assertions of the form "X is a categorically required choice" are meaningless, i.e., could never be true. Either moral understanding is logically independent of the comprehensive comparative variable or choices can never be morally evaluated—or "value-free" theory is impossible. For the sake of clarity, I should note that this conclusion cannot be escaped by asserting that the comprehensive moral principle might be different than the comprehensive variable by virtue of which human choice is understood. Identifying categorically required choices is, in this respect, understanding human choices, so that the putative difference would yield two correct understandings of human choice as such. There can only be one variable in accord with which human choice alternatives are comprehensively compared. I will call (i) and (ii) alternative claims to a comprehensive moral principle, and I will argue that the comprehensive comparative variable is morally evaluative by showing that neither of these alternative claims can be true.

First Alternative Claim

The first of these two may be refuted by pursuing tenaciously the fact that understanding or identifying categorically required choices requires a morally comparative variable. To say that some choice alternative is categorically required does not simply assert that this alternative displays some descriptive characteristic. This is the fundamental point generally summarized in the distinction between description and evaluation. Moral status is attributed to a choice alternative because of (or, at least, in addition to) the descriptive characteristics it displays; given what it is, one then also concludes that it is categorically required. This difference may also be expressed by saying that "categorically required" identifies not a difference in the description of choices but a *difference with respect to choosing*. Moreover, this last formulation of the point clarifies why the identification of morally required choices requires a comparative variable, i.e., because a moral claim asserts that categorically required alternatives differ from others precisely in being categorically required. Moral claims, in other words, identify objective or categorical similarities and differences with respect to choosing, and this identification is a comparison of choice alternatives in that respect. Given, then, that "categorically required" does not identify a descriptive characteristic, the variable by virtue of which these similarities and differences are specified must be a variable with respect to choosing, or a morally evaluative variable.

It should be emphasized that the moral variable must be one of which all of the choice alternatives in question are instances in similar or differing ways. Consider a simplified but representative illustration in which the agent must choose between telling the truth and lying. To say that the agent ought to tell the truth implies a categorical difference between these two alternatives with respect to choosing, such that the former is categorically superior in this respect. What is implied in this claim? I have argued earlier that human self-understanding implies a positive or determinate comparison between the alternatives, such that human activity may be understood as X rather than Y, and that this positive comparison implies a comparative variable of which both alternatives are instances. Accordingly, the difference between truth-telling and lying is understandable in terms of a variable of which both are instances. Now it is claimed that truth-telling is properly understood as categorically required. Human self-understanding, therefore, implies that this choice alternative *in this respect* may be compared with the alternative of lying, so that the two must be instances of a comparative variable with respect to choosing.

This point, which is pivotal to the present argument, may be confirmed by entertaining the contradictory position. It might be objected that truth-telling does not need to be determinately or positively compared to lying *with respect to choosing*. According to this objection, truth-telling simply is categorically required or superior with respect to choosing, and to say that the other choice alternative is morally inferior is simply to say that it is not truth-telling. There is no positive comparison between the alternatives because the proscribed alternative enters the moral evaluation simply by virtue of what it is not. We may call this the "intuitionist objection," since it might be affirmed by some ethical intuitionists, who hold that "categorically required" is a "non-natural" or, at least, "simple" property which can be apprehended only by direct inspection (see, e.g., Moore, 1903).

But the problem is that this objection implies the positive comparison which it attempts to deny, because it assumes that the moral evaluation which has been asserted is understandable, in the sense that it is true and, therefore, can be verified or justified. If "truth-telling is categorically required" is justifiable, then "lying is categorically required" must be falsifiable. ("Lying is categorically permissible" must also be falsifiable, but given the point at issue here, we need not add this complication.) Since lying is a positive choice alternative, "lying is categorically required" is falsifiable only if the positive characteristics of the alternative are incompatible with or, at least, other than the characteristic "categorically required." Negatives, in other words, imply positives, and if lying is not categorically required, this implies that lying is positively other than this characteristic. Nor will it change the matter to say that we apprehend the absence of the characteristic "categorically required" by direct inspection, because this can only mean that direct inspection reveals positive characteristics that are other than "categorically required." We know that a lemon is not red not because we apprehend the sheer absence of red but because we apprehend the presence of yellow and because yellow is other than red. If we apprehend nothing other than red, either we apprehend nothing at all or we apprehend a red thing. But if positive characteristics of lying are known to be other than "categorically required," then a positive comparison between the choice alternatives with respect to choosing is implied. A given choice alternative cannot enter a moral evaluation simply by virtue of what it is not, and the assertion that some choice is morally required implies a positive comparison between choice alternatives. For instance, categorically required might mean "superior with respect to enhancing human well-being." Accordingly, truth-telling may be compared with the positive characteristics of lying in terms of the variable "enhancing human well-being," such that lying is known to be inferior in this respect and thus other than "categorically required."

More generally, one may conclude that any understanding of categorical similarities and differences with respect to choosing requires a morally evaluative variable of which the similarities and differences in question are instances. In turn, this implies that the alternatives in *all* possible situations of human choice must be instances of one or another morally evaluative variable. To this it might be objected that some situations of human choice are not moral ones, that there is no choice alternative or class of alternatives which is categorically required. One might say that Frost's choice of whether to take the less traveled or the well-worn path is not a situation of moral choice, although the choice of whether to make the trip may have been so (depending upon the alternatives, i.e., the situation, at the time). One need not assert that Frost was morally required to choose one path or the other in order to refute this objection. Granted that he was not, still the identification of choices that are morally indifferent, in distinction from those of moral choice, itself implies a moral comparison. For this identification asserts that certain differences among situations of choice make a categorical difference with respect to choosing; in one kind of situation, the alternatives are morally indifferent, in the other they are not. This assertion requires a moral comparison of the situations. The claim that Frost's alternative paths are morally indifferent is itself a moral claim and implies a morally evaluative variable in accord with which this situation is distinguished from situations of moral choice. What has been said in the previous paragraph regarding the comparison of alternatives *within* a given situation is also true, mutatis mutandis, of a comparison *between* situations. If a moral conclusion is justified, a moral comparison is implied. All possible human choice alternatives are instances of some one or another morally evaluative variable.

It is evident that the morally evaluative variable for any situation of human choice cannot itself be a matter of choice. Were it the case that one is morally bound to tell the truth only if one chooses an evaluative variable according to which truth-telling is required, then truth-telling would be hypothetically required, required if the human in question simultaneously chooses so to evaluate his or her choices. To the contrary, "categorically required" means "required independently of any condition that is simultaneously chosen by the human in question." This is just to repeat that moral evaluations advance reasons for the choice that are independent of the choice, so that the morally evaluative variable must be *objective*.

It also follows from what has been said that there must be a *supreme* morally evaluative variable, a single principle of which all possible human choice alternatives are instances, such that it provides the terms in which all categorical similarities and differences with respect to choosing may be understood. A supreme principle, in other words, is a universal principle that is the only universal principle. There is substantial contention in ethical philosophy regarding this claim, and the argument for it must consider two possible counterclaims: (a) At least one choice may be categorically required without being so identified in terms of a universal moral principle. (b) There may be more than one universal moral principle.

A claim that (a) is the case may be called the "relativist objection," because it implies a kind of moral relativism, at least with respect to the choice or choices in question. Since the choice may be categorically required without being so identified by a universal moral principle, it must be moral solely by virtue of a morally evaluative variable that is more or less contextual or relative to specific conditions which the choice in question illustrates. In taking issue with such relativistic moral principles, I do not mean to deny that conditions of choice vary widely, so that there may be more or less specific morally evaluative variables relative to different situations of human choice. The keeping of one's promises may be categorically required only given specific conditions. What is categorically required in one culture or one historical age may in specific respects differ from what is so required in another. But to say that one or more morally evaluative variable is *relative* does not mean that it is *relativistic*, in that sense that moral choices may be identified without a universal moral principle. For the claim that some relative principle identifies moral choices always implies the nonrelative moral claim that specific conditions in which the relative principle applies make a categorical difference with respect to choosing. To say, as some might, that democratic principles properly apply to the conduct of political affairs only given the precondition of a certain level of economic production is, first, to identify specific economic conditions in distinction from other situations of human choice and, second, to claim that these differences make a categorical difference with respect to choosing. Identifying the distinct conditions requires a comparative variable, and identifying these conditions as morally significant requires a moral comparison. The relative variable requires a more general morally evaluative variable. If this more general variable is also relative, the same considerations apply to it. Nor can a nonrelative principle be avoided by claiming that moral evaluation involves an infinite regress of relative moral principles. For the more general principle is a necessary condition for identifying the morally evaluative character of the more specific variable, so that an infinite regress of relative principles would imply that no categorically required choices can be identified. Because moral conclusions require moral comparisons, a relative moral principle could not be identified as such in the absence of a universal moral principle.

It is worth noting that any relativistic moral claim implies that all moral claims are relativistic. If some specified moral choices are identified solely by virtue of a given relative variable, then all other moral choices are identified by other variables that are also relative because they exclude the choices initially specified. If one moral choice is not identified by a universal principle, in other words, there can be no universal moral principle. If, as I argued earlier, all human choice alternatives must be instances of some morally evaluative variable, it follows that all are instances of some relativistic moral principle. The relativist objection, we may say, implies general moral relativism, and the argument against (a) is simply that general moral relativism *is* a nonrelative moral claim. For it identifies, or implies an identification of, the specific differences that make a categorical difference with respect to choosing. Because the comparison of different situations of human choice with respect to morally relevant differences is a moral comparison, relative moral variables imply a nonrelative or universal moral principle.

This conclusion means that the universal moral principle in question must be exceptionless. Thus, the relativist objection may be reconsidered by reformulating it in these terms. J. B. Schneewind, for instance, has argued that required choices do not require exceptionless principles. To the contrary, he says, moral principles, as legal ones, "may have to do with rebuttable subsumptions" (Schneewind, 251). An acceptable moral principle gives a reason for doing the act which it prescribes. Because the principle is exceptionable, however, "it is open to an objector to give reasons for thinking the case in question to be exceptional, but if no such reasons are given, then the act dictated by the principle remains the act that ought to be done. . . . In the absence of definite grounds for thinking the particular case exceptional it would be foolish to take the logical possibility of its being exceptional [i.e., the logical fact that the principle is exceptionable] as a serious reason for doubting that it ought to be done" (251). One may grant that an acceptable and exceptionable moral principle applies in the absence of reasons to the contrary. But the issue Schneewind does not settle is how one might know when reasons to the contrary have been found. Properly "thinking the case in question to be exceptional" requires *moral* reasons, i.e., reasons to think that some action other than the one prescribed by the principle is at least morally permissible, and such reasons entail a morally evaluative variable other than the exceptionable principle with which one began.

The claim to exception requires a moral comparison between the action prescribed by that principle and some alternative action; only so can it be known that the differences between them do not constitute in favor of the former a categorical difference with respect to choosing, so that the alternative action is at least morally permissible. An exceptionable principle implies another variable in terms of which the exceptions are compared with cases to which the principle applies; it implies another principle of higher generality and of which the first is a specification. It might be questioned why the second principle must be of higher generality than the first. It might be said that cases of exception for one moral principle are identified when there are circumstances in which a second principle of similar or lesser generality happens to dictate an alternative choice and the first principle is not morally "overriding." But to know that the first principle is not overriding requires a morally evaluative variable in accord with which cases of the first are compared with cases of the second, a variable of which both sets of cases are instances. A principle of higher generality of which both of the other two are specifications is implied.

For reasons already given, moral evaluation cannot involve an infinite regress of exceptionable principles. Since the more general principle is a necessary condition for identifying exceptions to (and therefore the applicability of) the more specific principle, the former is required in order to know what counts as "reasons to the contrary," so that the logical possibility of the first principle being exceptionable would indeed leave "serious reason for doubting" that the act it prescribes ought to be done. An infinite regress of exceptionable principles, then, would imply that no categorically required choices can be identified. The claim that all moral principles are exceptionable is an *exceptionless* claim. It is, moreover, an exceptionless *moral* claim, because it implies a comparison of choice alternatives by virtue of which the exceptions and applications of each exceptionable principle are identified—a comparison with respect to choosing. But the more direct way to say this is to repeat that a comparison of all human choices is required in order to know that a putative exceptionable principle has any applicability, that it is indeed a moral principle.

Granting, however, that all moral principles cannot be exceptionable, it might then be asserted that there is no single exceptionless principle of which all choice alternatives are instances. Perhaps there are two or more exceptionless principles, each of which applies to certain kinds of cases, such that cases to which any one applies are never cases to which another applies. But this change cannot redeem the position. A diversity of exceptionless principles implies a comparison between the cases to which one applies and those to which another applies in order to identify what principle applies to what cases. Whether all principles are said to be exceptionable or some are exceptionless, general moral relativism implies a nonrelative or universal moral variable of highest generality in accord with which the morally significant similarities and differences of different cases of human choice are understood.

Still, in opposition to a supreme moral variable, it might be said that (b) there is more than one morally evaluative variable of which all choice alternatives are instances. This may be called the "pluralist objection," because the claim is that neither or none of the two or more such variables are specifications of any other, and all choices must be evaluated in terms of all such moral principles. William K. Frankena, for instance, has argued that beneficence and justice are two such principles (see Frankena, 43–52). But if the two or more principles were indeed different, then situations of choice would be possible in which the moral alternative identified by one principle is different than the alternative identified by another. Since one cannot choose both alternatives, one would have to choose between or among the principles in order to identify what is categorically required in such a situation. But "categorically required" means "required independently of any condition that is simultaneously chosen by the human in question." Another variable is required in order to compare the cases to which each of the others is relevant and thereby to identify objectively which principle, if either, is overriding in such cases of conflict, and this is just to say that the two or more principles in question imply a supreme moral variable.

Against this argument that two conflicting principles require a third in accord with which the conflict is properly adjudicated, Brian Barry has urged that "choices on the basis of principles which are not all reducible to a single one" are rational "provided only that the (actual or hypothetical) choices made show a consistent pattern of preference" (Barry, 4). But to say that the exercise of a consistent pattern of preference constitutes rationality (is justifiable) in such cases of conflict is to say that the differences between the alternative choices make no categorical difference with respect to choosing, since any consistent pattern of preference is permissible. The claim that the choices which two or more principles prescribe are categorically similar with respect to choosing is a comparison that entails a morally evaluative variable other than the principles that conflict. More generally stated, whatever implicit or explicit claim is made with respect to the differing choices which the differing principles prescribe involves a moral comparison between these choices. Thus, there can be only one morally evaluative variable of which all choice alternatives are instances; there must be a supreme moral principle.[1]

If the preceding discussion has shown that "X is a categorically required choice" implies a supreme moral principle, it has also given reason to say that this principle must be *comprehensive*, must compare all choices *in all aspects*. The latter may be explicitly argued by supposing it is not the case, and this supposition may be called the "partialist objection," because it asserts that the supreme moral variable compares some but not all aspects (parts) of choices. Some might hold that human activity is morally evaluated only insofar as it affects or intends to affect human individuals other than the agent. Thus, the affects or intended affects of activity upon the agent or upon nonhuman existence are morally indifferent, unless they have or may have further consequences for other humans. Similarly, the partialist objection is implicit in all theories of established liberalism. Because these theories assert that human self-interests are solely matters of preference, they imply that choices are not morally evaluated in this aspect. Friedman and Gewirth conclude that choices are morally compared only insofar as they affect or intend to affect the distribution of certain generic capacities.

But the dictum is now clear: moral conclusions involve moral comparisons. Were the supreme moral principle partial, it would imply that the aspects of choices which it does not compare make no categorical difference, that is, are categorically similar, with respect to choosing. In the established liberal form of the objection, the implied claim is the following: insofar as choices have to do with self-interest, as opposed to the distribution of certain generic capacities, those choices are categorically similar with respect to choosing. Again, however, that im-

1. Schneewind also argues against the need for a conflict-resolving supreme principle. "Just as there are good reasons for believing each of two incompatible factual assertions, so there may be good reasons for doing each of two incompatible actions. We may be in a position in which we are unable to tell which of two assertions—if either of them—is really true and we may be similarly unable to tell for which of the two actions—if either—there are ultimately better reasons" (Schneewind, 252). But surely this analogy does not show what Schneewind intends. That we are unable to tell which of the two assertions (if either) is really true does not compromise the point that both cannot be true. We may indeed find ourselves in a situation wherein we are unsure for which of two actions there are ultimately better reasons. But this does not compromise the point that there cannot be ultimately better reasons for both. Either one or the other is categorically required, or either action is permissible, or there are ultimately better reasons for some third alternative. In any case, a moral comparison of the alternatives in question is implied; a morally evaluative variable by which the conflict may be resolved is required. Schneewind then argues that, in any event, this conflict-resolving principle need not be supreme, to use my term, or "the first principle of morality," to use his (252). But this is tantamount to claiming that the conflict-resolving principle may be exceptionable, and here I refer the reader to my previous discussion.

plication *is* a categorical comparison of those aspects with respect to choosing and, therefore, compares in terms of their moral relevance the aspects supposedly not compared. Only a *comprehensive* variable in terms of which human choices as such are compared could identify categorically required choices. But a variable in terms of which human choice alternatives as such are compared can be nothing other than the comprehensive variable according to which human choice as such is understood.

It follows from this line of thought that the first of the two alternative claims, one of which must be true if human activity does not imply a comprehensive moral principle, is not true. On the contrary, if some choices may be categorically required, the comprehensive comparative variable for correctly understanding human activity is morally evaluative of human choices. Difference in terms of that variable is a categorical difference with respect to choosing. If, with hedonist psychology, "pleasure of the agent" is the variable through which human activity is correctly understood, choice alternatives may differ with respect to the measure in which they contribute to the agent's pleasure, and, if the notion of moral choice is meaningful, then difference with respect to the agent's pleasure is a categorical difference with respect to choosing. Those alternatives which are superior in terms of the comprehensive comparative variable (in the case of hedonism, those which maximize the agent's pleasure) are categorically required and those which are inferior are categorically proscribed. Within any given situation of human choice, one is morally required to choose that alternative, or to choose from among that class of alternatives, that is superior in terms of the comprehensive comparative variable, and all other alternatives are categorically proscribed.[2]

Second Alternative Claim

"Value-free" theories of human activity, which hold that human activity does not imply a comprehensive moral principle, are now left with the second of the two alternative claims mentioned earlier: putative asser-

2. Since I have concluded that comparative inequality means *some* categorically required alternative, it might be objected that the most inferior alternative could be the one categorically required. This solution entails that alternatives are to be evaluated in terms of the relative absence of something, of the content compared according to the comprehensive variable. In turn, this implies that the content of the variable has no value, precisely because its presence in human activity should be minimized; but the claim that something is valueless must be based upon some claim regarding what is valuable, and since the basis for evaluation is the comprehensive variable in question, this solution makes it impossible to determine what is valuable. Thus, the solution is untenable. In matters of evaluation, negatives imply positives. Since the only basis for positive evalua-

tions of the form "X is a categorically required choice" are meaningless, could never be true. It is for this reason that such theories (at least, those among them which do not hold to the complete other-determination of human activity) generally affirm what may be called "the preference theory of human choice." This view may be distinguished from the established liberal view of happiness. Although the latter holds that self-interest is solely a matter of preference, it also affirms that "X is a categorically required choice" is meaningful, because it asserts one or another moral principle by virtue of which the opportunity for pursuing self-interest is properly distributed. In contrast, the preference theory of human choice denies all putative moral principles. Not only choices of self-interest, but all choices in all aspects are solely matters of preference. In no sense, then, can human choices be called morally good or bad (or right or wrong), and to say this is to assert that "X is a categorically required choice" is meaningless.

In order for the preference theory to be true, the putative assertion "X is a categorically required choice" must be either hopelessly vague or self-contradictory. These alternatives exhaust the relevant class of meaningless assertions. If a putative assertion combines concepts each of which is sufficiently clear to be used in meaningful assertions (i.e., is not hopelessly vague), then the assertion in question is itself meaningless only if the combination of concepts is logically impossible or self-contradictory. Given what has been said earlier in this chapter about the meanings of "choice" and "categorically required," I presume that "X is a categorically required choice" is not hopelessly vague. It remains to ask, then, whether this assertion is self-contradictory. An affirmative answer to this question is possible only if the assertion in question includes or implies two meaningful assertions which are inconsistent. "X is a married bachelor" is self-contradictory because it includes or implies two meaningful assertions ("X is married" and "X is a bachelor") which are inconsistent.

Is "X is a categorically required choice" similarly self-contradictory? To immediate appearances, there is nothing inconsistent in saying that one has a certain choice alternative and that this alternative is required independently of any condition that is itself chosen by the human in question. However, it might be argued that, at least with respect to choices, "X is categorically required" implies that some other alternative, Y, is categorically proscribed, and, this argument concludes, a categorically proscribed choice is impossible. But this argument fails if the

tion is the variable in question, superiority in terms of the variable must identify the alternative that is categorically required.

following two conditions obtain: first, if there is a way to distinguish between categorically required and categorically proscribed choices, and, second, if it is possible for an agent to choose what is categorically proscribed. That the first of these conditions obtains has been suggested in the immediately preceding discussion; categorical differences with respect to choosing may be distinguished in terms of the comprehensive comparative variable according to which human choice as such is correctly understood. That the second condition obtains follows from the fact that distinctively human activity is, or at least involves, a self-understanding. Self-conscious activity includes the capacity to choose a false self-understanding. Humans may choose to understand themselves in terms of a variable taken to be comprehensive although in truth it is not. If this variable is morally evaluative, humans may thereby choose what is in truth categorically proscribed.

Perhaps, then, "X is a categorically required choice" is meaningless because "X is categorically required" is inconsistent with some assertion implied in "X is a choice." In other words, perhaps "X is a choice" implies "X is a Z," such that this latter assertion is inconsistent with "X is categorically required." Just so, I argued earlier, "X is a completely other-determined, self-conscious activity" is meaningless, because self-consciousness implies self-determination in some measure. But there can be no such characteristic, Z, entailed in the meaning of "choice," because the assertion "X is categorically required" asserts an objective difference *with respect to choosing* and, therefore, *assumes* whatever other characteristics choices may have. Given whatever other similarities and differences there may be, the assertion at issue claims only that choices may also differ with respect to choosing. As I mentioned earlier, it is precisely this absence of inconsistency which is generally summarized as the distinction between evaluation and description. Evaluation is not a competitive description; consequently, it cannot be inconsistent with any possible description that choice alternatives may have. Because of this distinction, a comparison of human choices with respect to morally relevant differences is always a moral comparison. In any event, it follows that the assertion "X is a categorically required choice" is meaningful, and the preference theory is false.

I conclude that neither of the following two claims can be true: (i) Although assertions of the form "X is a categorically required choice" are meaningful, the identification of these choices does not require a comparison of human choice as such. (ii) Assertions of the form "X is a categorically required choice" are meaningless. Thus, the claim "the comprehensive comparative variable is not morally evaluative" also cannot be true, and its contradictory, "the comprehensive comparative variable *is* morally evaluative," must be true. Precisely because the notion of categorical similarities and differences with respect to choosing presumes any other similarities and differences which choice alternatives may have, assertions of the form "X is a categorically required choice" are meaningful. For the same reason, the identification of categorical similarities and differences with respect to choosing requires a comparison in this respect of choice alternatives as such. Accordingly, the comprehensive comparative variable in terms of which human choice as such is correctly understood *is* a comprehensive evaluative principle in terms of which moral choices are identified. Superiority in terms of the comprehensive comparative variable identifies an alternative as categorically required, and this conclusion is entailed by the self-conscious character of human activity.

This does not imply that no human choices are matters of preference. It is certainly possible that some or all of the alternatives in a given situation of choice are, in light of the comprehensive variable, comparatively equal. In that event, there is no difference with respect to choosing. But matters of preference never arise because the alternatives are neither good nor bad, i.e., choices cannot be *solely* a matter of preference. Since the alternatives are equal in light of an evaluative comparison—are *evaluated* as equal—the proper use of the term "preference" in relation to human activity is to say that in some situations choice from among a class of alternatives is morally required, the choices within that class all being equally good or right, so that we are morally permitted to choose among them as we prefer.

The Argument Reviewed

Human activity, I have argued, entails a comprehensive moral principle, such that the variable in terms of which human choice alternatives are comprehensively understood is morally evaluative. If this is so, it follows that the established liberal or preferential view of happiness cannot be true. This is not because established liberalism asserts the preference theory of human choice, the *second* of the two claims that are alternatives to a comprehensive moral principle. As the theories of Friedman and Gewirth illustrate, established liberalism always affirms one or more moral principles in accord with which the opportunity to pursue happiness ought to be distributed and insofar denies the preference theory of human choice. But just because such liberalism does include a preferential view of those wants or interests for which opportunity should be morally distributed, it asserts the *first* of the two claims that are alternatives to a comprehensive moral principle: although assertions of the form "X is a categorically required choice" are meaningful (may be true), the identification of these choices does not require a comparison of human choice as such. Of course, to say that established liberalism is committed to this claim is another way of saying that such liberalism excludes a moral criterion in accord with which self-interests may be evaluated, so that moral claims refer solely to the proper relations among individuals of whose self-interests those claims are logically independent. The argument invalidates established liberalism because it also concludes that partialism is a fallacy. Since self-conscious activity entails a comprehensive moral principle, it is always fallacious to assert that human activity may be moral in part but is nonmoral as a whole. This assertion claims that the aspects of activity which are not morally evaluated make no categorical difference with respect to choosing, and that claim implies a moral evaluation of those aspects. Established liberalism, which claims that self-interests are not morally evaluated, is partialist, and the theories of Friedman and Gewirth are indeed instances of a fallacy.

The fact that the first alternative is false does not necessarily invalidate the preferential view of happiness. Self-interest could still be solely a matter of preference, but only on condition that the second alternative is true, that *all* human choice is solely a matter of preference. Thus, we arrive generally at the conclusion to which the critical discussion of Gewirth's theory specifically led: if self-interest is solely a matter of preference, humans necessarily act in a world in which each wars against all, because there are no categorically required choices. But I have also argued that the second alternative is false, so that human activity entails a comprehensive moral principle.

The argument has further sought to keep a promise issued in chapter 1, that I would show why all theories of human associations are informed, implicitly or explicitly, by normative principles or moral commitments, so that the intent to formulate a "value-free" theory cannot be fulfilled. If human activity entails a comparative variable in accord with which human choice as such is understood, the two alternative claims to a comprehensive moral principle constitute the only possible grounds for a "value-free" theory of human activity. If both of these claims are false, so that the comprehensive comparative variable is morally evaluative, then any theory of human activity is implicitly or explicitly committed to a moral principle. This follows because a theory of human activity, insofar as it is a theory, requires a comprehensive comparative variable by virtue of which all human activity is understood. Whatever is so asserted by a given theory is also implicitly asserted as a comprehensive moral principle. Because human activity entails a comprehensive moral principle, so does any theory thereof. It remains only to say that a theory of associations is necessarily a theory of the human activity which constitutes those associations, so that all political theories are implicitly or explicitly normative.

Finally, the argument in this chapter has set a formal condition for a convincing political theory, namely, that such theory must be informed by a comprehensive moral principle. Because this condition invalidates the preferential view of happiness, it follows that self-interest must be morally defined, so that a distinction between genuine and putative self-interest may be drawn. It also follows that an acceptable definition of happiness will be one that is implied by a comprehensive variable for understanding and evaluating human activity. In chapter 1, I defined reformed liberal theories as those which include some moral criterion or standard in accord with which an individual's genuine and putative self-interest may be distinguished. We may now say that a liberal theory which fulfills the formal condition defended in this chapter will have to be an instance of reformed, rather than established, liberalism.

Five

Reformed Liberalism
John Dewey

The discussion now turns to the thought of John Dewey in order to display a reformed liberal perspective on independent associations. Dewey was one of the few eminent American philosophers of the twentieth century. His achievement is distinctive, enduring, and comprehensive. "In many ways," writes John E. Smith, "Dewey was *the* American philosopher of the first half of this century" (Smith, 116). One reason to say this is Dewey's constitutive democratic purpose. "His guiding intention throughout an extraordinarily long and influential career," writes Robert Horowitz, "may be summarized as the attempt to further the realization of democracy in every sphere of life" (Horowitz, 746). For Dewey, philosophy is the attempt to formulate a democratic understanding of all human activities and, therefore, a democratic resolution to the general problems in human experience. Although this may be sufficient to justify Dewey's own claim that his political thought falls within the liberal tradition, it does not necessarily imply that his theory is an example of reformed liberalism. Friedman and Gewirth would also think themselves committed to the realization of democracy. The claim that Dewey's understanding of democracy differs by virtue of its moral definition of happiness or self-interest will have to be argued at the appropriate point in this chapter.

The Democratic Ideal

That a democratic ideal informs Dewey's philosophy reflects the fact that his thought is both empirical and pragmatic. In Dewey's reading, modern empirical science has created a revolution "enormous in scope," which has left unchanged "almost no detail of belief about nature" (1957, 53). The pivotal character of this revolution has been the increasing application of the method of inquiry which observes particular facts, formulates hypotheses regarding their explanation, and tests the hypotheses by experimentation (see, e.g., 1957, ix). The scientific revolution is, for Dewey, irreversible, so that philosophy must now proceed with free acceptance of "the standpoint and conclusions of modern science" (1958, ix). It follows, he believes, that philosophy should affirm the method of science as *the* method of intelligence, of thinking as such, and thus understand itself "from the analogy of empirical method in scientific inquiry" (1958, 31). "The theory of empirical method in philosophy does for experienced subject matter on a liberal scale what it does for special sciences on a technical scale," so that philosophy is "thinking at large" and "has its distinctive position in its generality" (1958, 2, 27, 398). For philosophy, as for science, "notions, theories, systems, no matter how elaborate or self-consistent they are, must be regarded as hypotheses" (1957, 145).

Philosophy is properly empirical because "the standpoint and conclusions of modern science" are the consequence of "the most revolutionary discovery yet made"—that what alone is "actually 'universal' is *process*" (1957, xiii). For science, the world is infinitely open and "infinitely variegated," so that "change rather than fixity is now a measure of 'reality' or energy of being; change is omnipresent" (1957, 61). This does not deny that there are more or less unchanging structures to be discovered; on the contrary, the world displays "correlations of change" or "constant orders of change" (1957, 61), although these correlations are themselves mutable in the infinite process and can only be apprehended by methodical attention to specific changes. Accordingly, the scientist "speaks of law where the ancients spoke of kind and essence" (1957, 61).

Dewey does not intend to say that philosophy excludes metaphysics, if one means by this "cognizance of the generic traits of existence" (1958, 51). But the proper metaphysics is precisely one of universal process, so that all things must be understood in terms of their place in the omnipresent course of change and, therefore, in relation to "their antecedent and contemporary connections" and "the consequences with respect to which . . . each acts and moves" (1954, 187). Thus, "qualitative individuality and constant relations" are "the common traits of all existence" (1958, 113). Individuals are defined by their relations. "An individual is a *distinctive* way of behaving in conjunction and *connection* with other distinctive ways of acting" (1954, 188). "There is no mystery about the fact of association, of an interconnected action which affects the activity of singular elements. There is no sense in asking how individuals come to be associated. They exist and operate in associations" (1954, 23). Dewey titles one of his books *Reconstruction in Phi-*

losophy (1957), because the metaphysics of change implied by the scientific revolution is, he holds, a fundamental reversal of traditional contemplative philosophy. For the latter, the end of thought is knowledge regarding "self-sufficient Being" (1958, 49) or eternal essences, which is assumed to be superior because it stands beyond uncertainty and change. The quest for such immutable or fixed forms is what Dewey calls the "philosophic fallacy" (see, e.g., 1930, 175), and his insistence upon avoiding this putative fallacy is what makes his philosophy empirical. Since another term for eternal or immutable forms is "necessary" being, one may say that Dewey's empiricism describes all things as "contingent individuals-in-association" or, more concisely, "contingencies-in-association."

Because Dewey's philosophy is empirical, it is also pragmatic. If philosophical notions and theories, like scientific ones, "must be regarded as hypotheses," philosophical inquiry requires an experimental test. In other words, "the hypothesis that works is the true one; and truth is an abstract noun applied to the collection of cases, actual, foreseen and desired, that receive confirmation in their works and consequences" (1957, 155–56). The appropriate test, Dewey holds, may be discerned once one realizes that philosophers, as humans generally, are also particular instances of contingency-in-association. As all other such individuals, humans must be understood in terms of their antecedent and contemporary connections and their consequences. In this sense, human experience is a part of nature. Human individuals are distinguished from all others, however, by their capacity for self-consciousness or intelligence; they alone are "beings who observe and think and whose ideas are absorbed by impulses and become sentiments and interests" (1954, 151). Similarly, associations become human when intelligent individuals interact, so that a common interest is consciously created and a "distinctive share in mutual action is consciously . . . claimed" (1954, 152) by each. Intelligence, in short, is the distinctively human way of existing contingently, and humans are intelligent contingencies-in-association or, as I will say henceforth, individuals-in-association. The exercise of intelligence, including philosophy, must be understood in terms of the contingent conditions to which human life is related and the consequences with respect to which it acts and moves. "Knowledge . . . is itself a modification of interactions" (1958, 414).

Because the conditions of human life are contingent, human existence, as all existence, is precarious; the world of which it is a part threatens as well as supports it. It is this uncertainty, Dewey believes, which lies behind the long-standing philosophical inclination to seek another world of fixed or self-sufficient being. Thereby, traditional philosophy illustrates that intelligence arises as a response to the problems which omnipresent change presents for human life. But this also means, in contrast to traditional philosophy, that the consequences with respect to which intelligence acts and moves can only be the common interests and distinctive shares therein at which individuals-in-association aim. The subject matter of thought, in other words, is human experience, and intelligence is an intervention between the problems presented in human experience and the possibilities of subsequent human experience. Dewey insists that "knowledge is relegated to a derived position, secondary in origin. . . . Knowledge is not something separate and self-sufficing, but is involved in the process by which life is sustained and evolved" (1957, 87). All thinking is "operational" or "instrumental to an active reorganization of the given environment, to the removal of some specific trouble and perplexity" (1957, 156). Thinking is for the sake of human practice.

Philosophy, as we have seen, is "thinking at large," so that it shares the problematic or practical character of all exercise of intelligence. "Philosophy grows out of and in intention is connected with, human affairs" (1957, xi). So understood, philosophy denies to metaphysics the pride of place that is granted to it by the traditional quest for self-sufficient forms. For "philosophy is love of wisdom" and "love of wisdom is concerned with finding its implications for the conduct of life, in devotion to what is good" (1958, 51). To identify contingency-in-association as the generic character of existence is simply to provide those "base lines to be used in more intricate triangulations" (1958, 413). The inclusive subject matter of philosophy is human experience "at large," and its principal task is to understand in general the contingent interactions of human life with its world and thereby to facilitate good human experience. If philosophy is to generality what science is to specificity, it follows that science is philosophically understood as one aspect of the conduct of life and that its final telos is practical. The empirical test of both scientific and philosophical hypotheses can only be their success in solving human problems or removing troubles and perplexities, or their contribution to good human experience. Hypotheses "work" or "receive confirmation in their consequences"—and thereby are true—insofar as they so contribute. Dewey's reconstruction in philosophy makes all thought instrumental to the "intentional reconstruction of experience" (1957, 134). Dewey's empiricism is also a pragmatism, and it may be called with equal justice either pragmatic empiricism or empirical pragmatism.

Empirical pragmatism seems to beg for a criterion of good human experience. But Dewey believes that this criterion is implicit in the position I have just summarized. If intelligence arises to solve problems in human experience, the "common purpose of men" is "nothing but the best, the richest and the fullest experience possible" (1958, 412). "Richest" and "fullest" imply that human experience is compromised by dissonance and loss and enhanced by increasing inclusiveness. "Those goods approve themselves, whether labelled beauty or truth or righteousness, which steady, vitalize and expand judgments in creation of new goods and conservation of old goods" (1958, 417). One may say that the notion of good human experience is implicit in what Dewey calls the "principle of continuity of experience" (1963b, 35). This principle states "that every experience both takes up something from those which have gone before and modifies in some way the quality of those that come after" (1963b, 35). Human experience is better, then, insofar as this continuity of experience is enhanced. As is well known, Dewey also calls the common purpose of human life "growth," i.e., growth in experience. "The end is no longer a terminus or limit to be reached. It is an active process of transforming the existent situation. . . . Growth is the only moral 'end'" (1957, 177; see also 1963b, 36f.).

Democracy is the term Dewey uses to universalize this moral "end." "Democracy has many meanings, but if it has a moral meaning, it is found in resolving that the supreme test of all human actions . . . shall be the contribution they make to the all-around growth of every member of society" (1957, 186). In its moral meaning, of course, democracy is an ideal for individual action and for associational life. Indeed, because humans are individuals-in-association, we may say that the telos of individuals is associations whose telos is the growth of all individuals. It is also apparent why Dewey's "guiding intention may be summarized as the attempt to further the realization of democracy in every sphere of life" (Horowitz, 746). The realization of democracy is one formulation of the final criterion by which all empirical hypotheses, all claims to truth, may be pragmatically tested; it is the common purpose at which all intelligence aims. If Dewey's reconstruction in philosophy makes all thought instrumental to the intentional reconstruction of experience, it is a "reconstruction . . . in the interest of democracy" (Horowitz, 747).

It is apparent that democracy in this sense is not simply a form of government. It is rather "the democratic idea in its generic social sense" (1954, 147). Dewey's extended definition is as follows: "From the standpoint of the individual, it consists in having a responsible share according to capacity in forming and directing the activities of the groups to which one belongs and in participating according to need in the values that the groups sustain. From the standpoint of groups, it demands liberation of the potentialities of members of a group in harmony with the interests and goods which are common. Since every individual is a member of many groups, this specification cannot be fulfilled except when different groups interact flexibly and fully in connection with other groups" (1954, 147). The democratic ideal, as I will call it, envisions human associations and associations of associations in which individuals participate according to capacities and needs that are finally to be specified in terms of the all-around growth or continuity of experience of every member of society.

Democracy as a form of government may be derived from democracy as a generic social ideal. If the diverse associations within a society should interact "flexibly and fully," this implies that those associations might fail to fulfill this ideal. From this circumstance, the function of the state arises. Its character may be understood through a distinction between private and public, and this distinction rests in turn upon the difference between direct and indirect consequences of associated activity. Association has consequences for the individuals who consciously control it. Insofar as its important consequences are limited to those individuals "directly engaged," it is private. Insofar as important consequences extend to others "who do not directly share in the performance of acts" (1954, 35), those so affected constitute a public. "Those indirectly and seriously affected for good or for evil form a group distinctive enough to require recognition and a name. The name selected is The Public" (1954, 35).

This group requires recognition not simply by the political theorist but especially by the participants. The distinctive character of human association is that consequences are consciously directed. In order to be human, the public must recognize itself and seek some control over the initial activity with which it is indirectly associated. Since the public is not directly engaged in the activity, its "control over the actions . . . must occur by some indirect means" (1954, 35). When the public organizes itself in order to supervise and regulate the indirect consequences, and thereby care for its interest, it is a state—and "the obvious external mark" of the public's organization is "the existence of officials" to act on the public's behalf, that is, the existence of government (1954, 27). The state is a "secondary form of association," whose officers "may act so as to fix conditions under which *any* form of association operates" (1954, 71–72). This does not necessarily mean that the state is restricted to the prevention of trespass or the resolution of conflicts among other associations. On the contrary, full and flexible interaction in the associational order implies that "the line between private and public is to be drawn on the basis of the extent and scope of the consequences of acts which are so important as to need control, whether by inhibition *or by promotion* (1954, 15, emphasis added). Of course, democratic forms of government, through which the public "shares in selecting its governors and determining their policies" (1954, 146), are required in order to assure that individuals in the public participate according to capacity and need, or so that "the interest of the public" will be the "supreme guide and criterion of governmental activity" (1954, 146).

For the sake of clarity, it should be said that Dewey's analysis of the public and its government suggests that a different public exists, which might organize itself into a different state and constitute a different government, each time that associated activity has important indirect consequences. To the best of my knowledge, he never discusses explicitly the move from this condition to one in which there is a single state and government for a given society or given arena of associational life. But clearly his intent is to assert that all members of the society are members of *the* public insofar as any are affected by important indirect consequences, and *the* government is to be so constituted as to care for all interests so affected.

It should also be noted that Dewey's understanding of the state is curiously partial. Clearly the democratic ideal, which requires that individuals participate in associations according to capacity and need, suggests that the state might have some function in regulating the *direct* consequences of human association. In practice, for instance, the state generally prohibits breach of contract and racial discrimination. While it may be true that such activities usually have important indirect consequences, we do not say (and presumably Dewey would not) that state regulation is here justified solely because of such indirect effects. It is also the consequences for one or more of the people "directly engaged" which are thought to warrant governmental regulation.

This curiosity, I think, can itself be understood. Given Dewey's commitment to empiricism and his aversion to fixed forms or essences, and given a recognition that states or governments have not always existed in human life as differentiated associations, he sought an empirical explanation for their emergence. This kind of explanation was achieved when he decided that differentiated states appeared because human society reached such complexity that those affected in an important way were not more or less directly engaged and could not directly care for their interests. Having arrived at this empirical explanation, however, Dewey fails to say explicitly what is implicit in his political theory as a whole—that states, once they emerge because of important indirect consequences, also assume at least some of the control of direct consequences that was previously left entirely to participants. In any event, this amendment does not alter the fact that the state involves those indirectly associated and, therefore, is an indirect instrument of control. The government takes action in relation to the direct consequences of other associations only because individuals other than those directly engaged believe that intervention is justified. In that sense, the government's care always involves a public, if not a public indirectly affected at least a public indirectly responsible. It remains that the state is a secondary form of association through which the public fixes conditions under which any form of association operates.

Contemporary Associations

Because Dewey holds that political thought, like all thought, is a pragmatic response to problematic conditions, one would expect that his theory of associations is properly understood as a response to the general problems of contemporary community life. Moreover, because the democratic ideal is one formulation of the pragmatic telos of all thought, political theory may be understood as the inclusive philosophical enterprise. Thus, Dewey holds that the "problems and subject matter of philosophy grow out of the stresses and strains in the community life in which a given form of philosophy arises." By his reading, the most general contemporary problematic in human associational life is the disparity between the physical and the distinctively human; or, since "any inquiry into what is deeply and inclusively human enters perforce into the specific area of morals" (1957, xxvi), between the physical and the moral.

In relation to the physical (including the physiological) world, modern society is committed to the methods and conclusions of science, and the consequences for community life are pervasive. "The present reach and thrust of what originates as science affects disturbingly every aspect of contemporary life, from the state of the family . . . , through the fine as well as the industrial arts, into political and economic relations of associations that are national and international in scope" (1957, xx). The effects are disturbing because the scientific method has not yet been employed in thinking about the distinctively human. In these latter aspects of contemporary life, prescientific thought forms prevail. Instead of intelligence that deliberately begins with specific problems and forms hypotheses to be tested, thought about moral association continues its appeal to fixed and immutable conditions or ends. Moral thought persists in its commitment to "general notions under which specific situations are to be brought," "general answers supposed to have a universal meaning that covers and dominates all particulars" and which thereby "do not assist inquiry" but "close it" (1957, 188–89). Science has "partial and exaggerated effects" (1957, xxv) within the human community because its consequences are not themselves intelligently assessed. "The institutional conditions into which it enters and which determine its human consequences have not as yet been subjected to any serious, systematic inquiry worthy of being designated scientific" (1957, xxv), and this "extraordinary split" occasions the basic incompatibilities of "the present estate" (1957, xxviii–xxix). To reconstruct philosophy is nothing other than "to do for the development of inquiry into human affairs and hence into morals what the philosophers of the last few centuries did for promotion of scientific inquiry into physical and physiological conditions and aspects of human life" (1957, xxiii; see also xxvii, xxxv, xxxix); it is to make moral inquiry empirical and pragmatic.

The fixed or general notions of moral theory which stand in the way of and therefore require this reconstruction may be summarized as the idea of the "separate individual." "The real difficulty is that the individual is regarded as something *given*, something already there" (1957, 193). As a statement of this belief, Dewey is fond of citing a passage from John Stuart Mill: "Men in a state of society are still men; their actions and passions are obedient to the laws of individual human nature. . . . Human beings in society have no properties but those which are derived from, and may be resolved into, the laws of individual men" (for Dewey's citations, see 1963a, 40; 1954, 195). Individuals are separate, then, because they are the creators but not the creatures of their associations; "individuals . . . have a full-blown psychological and moral nature, with its own set laws, independently of their association with one another" (1963a, 40). Dewey referred to his own political philosophy as "liberal" in character, because he believed that it "reconstructed" the basic affirmations of liberalism. But reconstructed liberalism must be sharply distinguished from earlier liberalism, because the hallmark of earlier liberalism is the notion of the separate individual. It was this idea which supported the theory that government's sole end is "the protection of individuals in the rights which were theirs by nature," so that society is, save for voluntary associations, obstructive, and we reach "the celebrated modern antithesis of the Individual and the Social" (1954, 87).

Earlier liberalism, we might say, was initially a reflection in thought of a social movement through which modern empirical science invaded associational life. This movement included distinctively religious changes and was largely effective by means of distinctively economic changes (see 1954, 85), which together gave birth to "a revolt against established forms of government and the state" (1954, 86). Because these forms were closely tied to other major institutions (ecclesiastic, economic, educational) and were supported by tradition, the revolt became one against the established associational order as such. "Deeply tinged by fear of government" and "activated by a desire to reduce it to a minimum," the movement was characterized intellectually by the decision "to go back to the naked individual, to sweep away all associations as foreign to his nature save as they proceeded from his own voluntary choice" (1954, 86, 88). The notion of the separate individual was born, and democracy as an associational form was restricted to the process by which government is minimized. The influence of modern empirical science as a part of this movement occurred principally through the new technology which it made possible and the "great economic changes" (1954, 85) which thereby followed. "New powerful . . . opportunities and wants" were "limited by established political and legal practices" (1954, 89). As a reflection in thought, therefore, earlier liberalism was wedded to classical economics. The notion of separate individuals became the idea of autonomous individuals subject by nature to economic laws "which brought about harmony of personal effort and social benefit" (1954, 91), and democratic government was wedded to laissez-faire.

The development of technology and the industrial revolution it made possible have yielded nothing less than "a new era of human relationships," an era of "massive organizations and complicated interactions" (1954, 107) that finds its prototypical expression in the realm of large economic corporations. It is a situation of "corporateness for which history affords no parallel" (1962, 41). Moreover, "the forms of associated action characteristic of the present economic order are so massive and extensive that they determine the most significant constituents of the public" (1954, 107). Dewey claims that serious indirect consequences of associational life have become wholesale and complicated on an unprecedented scale and that this situation is predominantly constituted by the corporate economic order. That order so dominates the society as greatly to condition the character of all other associations—the family, the schools, the media, and government. The indirect consequences of the economic order are not democratic, in the generic sense of the term, because economic associations are directed by the pursuit of private profit. Dewey's political writings are replete with criticism of profit-seeking as the aim of economic activity in contemporary America. This is not philosophical opposition to capitalism; such opposition would be, for Dewey, complicity in fixed moral forms and ideas. But

Dewey does hold that the profit system has become antidemocratic in the contemporary situation of corporateness dominated by the economic order. On the one hand, there is sheer economic exploitation. "Financial and industrial power, corporately organized, can deflect economic consequences away from the advantage of the many to serve the privilege of the few" (1962, 115). On the other hand, because the economic order greatly conditions every part of a highly interdependent social order, its orientation toward profit has cultivated a society organized for private economic gain. "An economic individualism of motives and aims underlies our present corporate mechanisms, and undoes the individual" (1962, 59). Associational life is not constituted by common interests that liberate the distinctive capacities and serve the distinctive needs of individuals; rather, organizations have become principally instrumental to economic consumption. America has become a "pecuniary culture," where "quantification" and "standardization" characterize both institutions and the thought and emotion of individuals (see 1962, chap. 2). "It is not too much to say that the whole significance of the older individualism has now shrunk to a pecuniary scale and measure" (1962, 90).

It is now clear why, in Dewey's view, the basic stresses and strains of contemporary community life are occasioned by the disparity between the physical and the moral. Modern society is thoroughly committed to the scientific apprehension of the physical world. But as this apprehension has invaded associational life through technology, economic change, and a "new order of human relationships," there has been no scientific inquiry into the moral consequences, into the distinctively human aspects of modern life. Moral thought has been controlled by the prescientific notion of the separate individual. This failure in political philosophy has contributed to the disturbing social effects. It is true that earlier liberalism emerged as a reflection in thought of vast modern changes. Because human association is consciously controlled, however, ideas have consequences; after emerging, liberal theory "entered into subsequent strivings and had practical effect" (1954, 85). The notion of autonomous individuals, to whom government is alien and for whom the laws of the marketplace are "natural," has been used to legitimate a society that is instrumental to economic consumption and to protect from public supervision the rising corporate order in which distinctive individuals are thoroughly submerged (see 1954, 95; 1962, 51).

We return, then, to the claim that reconstruction in philosophy requires a formulation through which the scientific method is fully extended from physical to distinctively human affairs, and the stresses and strains of community life are thereby addressed. Dewey's insistence that human individuals, like all others, are contingencies-in-association reconstructs political philosophy precisely at the point where the pre-scientific basis of earlier liberalism has prevented an address to contemporary problems. Instead of the notion of the separate individual, Dewey advances the idea that humans are the creatures as well as the creators of their associations, and this idea opens human life for empirical inquiry into contingent conditions and consequences, that is, extends the scientific method into the moral realm.

Because Dewey's theory makes the scientific revolution complete, the specific changes in contemporary community life that intelligence, properly exercised, will recommend cannot be determined without considerably more detailed empirical inquiry. Thus, for instance, Dewey does not theoretically identify the proper kinds and extent of state activity. "Our hypothesis is neutral as to any sweeping implications as to how far state activity may extend" (1954, 73). Everything depends upon the extent to which consequences require indirect regulation by an organized public. "At one time and place, a large measure of state activity may be indicated and at another time a policy of *laissez-faire*" (1954, 74). Nonetheless, one may formulate a general measure by which to evaluate the state, namely, "the degree of organization of the public and the degree to which its officers are so constituted as to perform their function of caring for public interests" (1954, 33). Together with the empirical judgments Dewey offers about contemporary corporate society, this measure permits some conclusions regarding the directions required by the democratic ideal.

Because the "new era of human relationships" has developed without systematic inquiry into its complex and massive indirect consequences, its public effects are little understood. The public, as Dewey expresses it, has been driven into "eclipse" (see 1954, 110f.) and is unable to recognize itself. "The ramifications of the issues before the public are so wide and intricate, the technical matters involved are so specialized, the details are so many and so shifting, that the public cannot for any length of time identify and hold itself" (1954, 137). This problem is all the more profound because the same corporate forces which have formed the new era have created individuals attentive to things other than the public interest, principally to private economic gain and the rewards that it purchases. "The members of an inchoate public have too many ways of enjoyment, as well as of work, to give much thought to organization into an effective public" (1954, 138–39).

The only genuine solution to this problem is the quest for "cooperative intelligence" (1963a, 81; see also 1954, 155), for patient empirical inquiry into associational problems and their resolutions. "The crisis in democracy demands the substitution of the intelligence that is exemplified in scientific procedure for the kind of intelligence that is now accepted" (1963a, 73). Dewey emphasizes that this intelligence can only be *cooperatively* pursued and exercised. Contemporary public discussion is compromised by the view that "intelligence is an individualistic possession" (1963a, 71), such that "each individual is of himself equipped with the intelligence that is needed, under the guidance of self-interest, to engage in political affairs" (1954, 157). This idea, of course, simply expresses in relation to human thinking the earlier liberal notion of separate individuals. As a consequence, the public has paid little attention to the ways in which public belief is formed, leaving those in substantial measure to propagandists and exploiters of sentiment, who are generally in service to "pecuniary profit" (see 1954, 169, 181–82). Intelligence as "the habit of considering social realities in terms of cause and effect and social policies in terms of means and consequences" (1963a, 73) has its origin as well as its end in social cooperation (see 1963a, 67f). Intelligence, like human existence generally, is constituted by association. For this reason, education occupies a pivotal place in Dewey's political philosophy (see 1944). Indeed, he can say that the task "is first of all education, in the broadest sense of that term. Schooling is a part of the work of education, but education in its full meaning includes all the influences that go to form the attitudes and dispositions . . . , which constitute dominant habits of mind and character" (1963a, 58).

As might be expected, Dewey's model for the cooperative pursuit of intelligence and the formation of public belief is the scientific community at its best. "There is a movement in science which foreshadows, if its inherent promise be carried out, a more humane age. For it looks forward to a time when all individuals may share in the discoveries and thought of others, to the liberation and enrichment of their own experience" (1962, 154). In the scientific community at its best, the inquiry of each is enhanced by the discoveries of others; similarly, the "opinions and beliefs concerning the public presuppose effective and organized inquiry" (1954, 77). By the same token, "no scientific inquirer can keep what he finds to himself or turn it to merely private account without losing his scientific standing" (1962, 154); similarly, "a fact of community life which is not spread abroad so as to be a common possession is a contradiction in terms" (1954, 177). There can be no limit upon the commitment to free communication. Finally, the pursuit of public intelligence in this sense is not simply a means to greater democracy; it is also the realization of democracy. At its best, the scientific community—and, mutatis mutandis, the public—pursues a common interest in which distinctive individuals participate according to capacity and need.

The consequence of a widespread commitment to cooperative inquiry will be a public that increasingly recognizes itself and thereby moves out of "eclipse." Increased intelligence with respect to the indirect consequences of corporate society will yield increased public organization to care for the public interest. In other words, the stresses and strains of contemporary life require an extension of democratic government. Since the principal institutional cause of contemporary problems is a corporate order whose indirect consequences escape attention, considerably greater governmental supervision of economic activity will be required to realize a "social organization extending to all areas and ways of living, in which the powers of individuals . . . shall be fed, sustained and directed" (1963a, 31). This should include a "cooperative control of industry" (1962, 132) that is not necessarily governmental; indeed, voluntary agreement should effect the change wherever possible (see 1962, 118). But since the democratic ideal means in our time "the doom of an exclusively pecuniary-profit industry" (1962, 118) that is massive in scope, it seems apparent that public supervision in substantial measure cannot be avoided.

Dewey endorses a kind of socialism (see, e.g., 1962, 120). If this term is used theoretically, however, it is important to clarify that Dewey's thought differs from what socialism is commonly taken to mean. In common usage, the term usually intends a social order that is distinguished from American capitalism solely in its transference of decisions from the free market to the state or public policy. It is assumed that socialism, no less than contemporary capitalism, affirms a social order whose dominant purpose is to maximize economic benefits or the fulfillment of consumer preferences and, therefore, a social order distinguished solely by the institutional mechanism through which this end is pursued. But enough has been said to indicate that Dewey's critique of the American corporate order is far more radical.

Not least among the evidences of this is Dewey's claim that large economic corporations have so affected all associational life than "an economic individualism of motives and aims . . . undoes the individual" (1962, 59). More generally, Dewey's distance from socialism in the common sense is revealed throughout his discussion of earlier and reconstructed liberalism and "individualism old and new" (1962). The fundamental object of criticism therein is not an institutional mechanism but the view that individuality is realized in the process of enjoying economic gain, and this because that view reflects the idea of the "separate individual." Dewey advocates a "new individualism," so that he calls for "a form of social organization that should include economic activities and yet should convert them into servants of the development of the higher human capacities of individuals" (1963a, 31–32). Dewey's socialism calls for "public control of industry and finance for the sake of *social* values" (1962, 118, my emphasis), where "social" implies a telos for the community other than the maximal enjoyment by all of economic benefits.

The character of this telos is indicated when Dewey suggests that action and association should seek to maximize the content of human sharing or communication. "Capacity to endure publicity and communication is the test by which a pretended good is genuine or spurious," and association means "coming together in joint intercourse for the better realization of any form of experience which is augmented and confirmed by being shared" (1957, 205). Dewey asserts that the standard by which community life may be evaluated is given in the following questions: "How numerous and varied are the interests that are consciously shared? How full and free is the interplay with other forms of association?" (1944, 83). The telos of the social order, then, is an association of associations in which human individuals maximally inherit from and contribute to each other, and the democratic ideal, in which humans associate according to capacity and need, should be understood in this sense. "Every way of life that fails in its democracy limits the contacts, the exchanges, the communications, the interactions by which experience is steadied while it is also enlarged and enriched. The task of this release and enrichment is one that has to be carried on day by day. Since it is one that can have no end till experience itself comes to an end, the task of democracy is forever that of creation of a freer and more humane experience in which all share and to which all contribute" (1951, 394). It is no surprise that Dewey's model for democratic association is the scientific community at its best. In that community each individual is enhanced by what he or she inherits from others and by his or her intent maximally to contribute to others. Since science is the method of intelligence, the appropriateness of this model is no accident. Distinctively human sharing is, by definition, conscious or intelligent sharing, so that democracy can be nothing other than maximizing the content of intelligent association.

This interpretation should not be read to imply that Dewey disparages the material wealth and well-being which have been achieved in modern industrial societies. On the contrary, he insists that economic or material well-being is a precondition for the human communication that is the telos of the social order. "The ultimate place of economic organization in human life is to assure the secure basis for an ordered expression of individual capacity and the satisfaction of the needs of man in non-economic directions" (1963a, 88). Similarly, it is not the dominantly corporate character of modern society that is problematic. Dewey believes that the "new era of human relationships" could become a new age of democratic achievement. "The vast, innumerable and intricate currents of trans-local associations might be so banked and conducted that they will pour the generous and abundant meanings of which they are potential bearers into the smaller intimate unions of human beings living in immediate contact with one another" (1954, 212). His criticism of "material industrial civilization" is that corporate economic organization is pursued for the sake of private profit, such that maximal economic reward becomes the telos of the social order and human individuals are "standardized." But he argues that modern economic advance and its corporate institutions should be understood to offer unprecedented opportunity for human communication. We require, to repeat a remark of Dewey's already cited, "a form of social organization that should include economic activities but yet should convert them into servants of the development of the higher human capacities of individuals" (1963a, 31–32).

It follows from what has been said that human capacities are higher insofar as their exercise permits individuals more fully to enjoy the distinctiveness of others and more fully to contribute to others. Dewey calls for the "liberation of the values of intellectual, esthetic and companionship life" (1963a, 88). Communication is greater insofar as its purpose is not simply economic but consists in the common pursuit of ideas, aesthetic appreciation, and human community itself. For this reason, Dewey holds that "the depth and range of our problem . . . is that of making the material an active instrument in the creation of the life of ideas and art" and insists that we ask "whether work itself can become an instrument of culture and . . . whether the masses can share freely in a life enriched in imagination and esthetic enjoyment" (1962, 126, 125). The reorganized economy should be such that "those who are engaged in the outward work of production and distribution of economic commodities" have a "share—imaginative, intellectual, emotional—in directing the activities in which they physically participate" (1962, 132, 131). The prescribed social order is one in which the exercise of these capacities is maximized, and this is another expression of the democratic ideal.

We are now in a position to appreciate how fully Dewey intends his theory to affirm that humans are, by virtue of their contingency, constituted by their associations. Maximizing the content of human communication is meant to be nothing other than maximizing individuality-in-association. The more humans communicate with each other, the more each is "a *distinctive* way of behaving in conjunction and *connection* with other distinctive ways of acting" (1954, 188). So understood, the democratic ideal is meant to be fully consistent with Dewey's repudiation of the "separate individual" and, through it, of the "philosophic fallacy." Thorough consistency with the contingency of existence means that the democratic ideal permits the extension of empirical method into the full range of human affairs. Adherence to the democratic ideal would end the duplicity of the physical and the moral in the social order and thereby resolve the stresses and strains of contemporary community life. Dewey might say that his political theory, if acted upon, would itself be pragmatically justified by successfully addressing the general human problematic.

We may also appreciate the extent to which Dewey thinks he has reconstructed the "enduring values" of liberalism. These values, he says, are "liberty, the development of the inherent capacities of individuals made possible through liberty, and the central role of free intelligence in inquiry, discussion and expression" (1963a, 32). In the "new individualism," liberty is not the freedom from restraint to pursue economic benefits, but the freedom so to interact with others as to make a distinctive contribution to them, the opportunity to associate democratically. "Liberty is that secure release and fulfillment of personal potentialities which takes place only in rich and manifold associations with others: the power to be an individualized self and enjoying in its own way the fruits of association" (1954, 150). Similarly, intelligence is not the means to economic advantage but the capacity to associate democratically; democracy is nothing other than cooperative intelligence. Finally, the development of the inherent capacities of individuals is not the enjoyment of economic benefits but the realization of democratic association, "rich and manifold associations" in which individuality-in-association is maximized.

Community-Regarding Associations

The resources are now available to pursue the significant distinctions among associations in Dewey's theory and to formulate the implied understanding of independent associations. Governmental and nongovernmental associations are distinguished by virtue of the "second-order" character of the former. The state is constituted to fix conditions under which other forms of associational life operate. Given this task, the state is an association to which all individuals must belong and is, therefore, involuntary. Government is limited to caring for public interests, to regulating serious indirect consequences. As we have seen, this limitation may be quite generous. "The question of what transactions should be left as far as possible to voluntary initiative and agreement and what should come under the regulation of the public is a question of time, place and concrete conditions that can be known only by careful observation and reflective investigation" (1954, 193). In a time and place such as twentieth-century America, the dominant corporateness of the social order mandates an extension of public activity quite beyond the needs of less interdependent societies. Nonetheless, the limitation is important. For liberty is an enduring value of the democratic ideal; maximal individuality-in-association for all is maximal freedom for all. We may say that the telos of the social order is to maximize voluntary, democratic associations, so that involuntary associations are subservient to it. Accordingly, the distinction between governmental and nongovernmental associations is theoretically significant.

Within the class of nongovernmental associations, is there a significant class that is also noncommercial, that is distinct from whatever classes include commonplace American commercial institutions or their equivalents? Whatever the answer to this question, it is readily apparent that no such class is constituted by nonprofit organizations. Dewey criticizes fundamentally the economic order based upon profit-seeking. In the contemporary situation of dominant corporateness, he contends, the profit-seeking system has led to economic exploitation and, what is finally more important, has created a "pecuniary culture" in which standardization and conformity are characteristic. For both reasons, the system is antidemocratic. Indeed, Dewey so repudiates profit-seeking in our present society as to suggest that he advocates the elimination of all profit-seeking organizations. If that is the case, the distinction between profit-seeking and nonprofit institutions will not help to identify a class of independent associations, because all nongovernmental associations will be properly nonprofit.

On the other hand, it might well be said that Dewey's position does not necessarily lead to the elimination of profit-seeking entirely. That conclusion would require a more or less complete economic plan that attends both to the ideal of democracy and the facts of contemporary life. Dewey never attempted such a plan. Given his uncompromising adherence to the scientific method of hypothesis and experimentation as the method of intelligence, it would have been inappropriate for him to rule out in principle the possibility that some parts of the economy could be helpfully organized on a for-profit basis. He might have entertained, for instance, John Kenneth Galbraith's notion that areas of economic activity that do not lend themselves to large-scale organization are best ordered through a market system (see Galbraith). At the least, it is clear that the dominant corporate institutions of the economy could not be profit-seeking. "The doom of an exclusively pecuniary-profit industry" (1962, 118) is implied, so that the corporate economy must be reconstituted through some combination of cooperative control (voluntary agreement should affect the change wherever possible) and public organization. Since some of the reconstituted economy will be voluntary, equivalents of contemporary corporate industry will be nongovernmental and nonprofit. Thus, nonprofit organizations will not constitute a noncommercial class.

Strictly speaking, however, this conclusion has not yet been reached theoretically, because appeal has been made to Dewey's judgments about the specific character of and his proposals for the contemporary economic order. But the theoretical argument is implied. For it is a theoretical matter that the relevance of profit-seeking to economic organization (or, as another example, the extent of governmental activity) should be judged in light of specific contemporary conditions. The distinction between what can be known theoretically and what requires specific analysis, in other words, is itself a theoretical distinction. The distinction that we seek between independent and other nongovernmental associations is, of course, also theoretical. The fact that Dewey's theory leaves the significance of nonprofit institutions waiting upon empirical inquiry means that the difference between profit and nonprofit cannot be equivalent to the required distinction.

Dewey does not explicitly discuss commercial and noncommercial associations. We do know, however, that distinctions among nongovernmental associations can be significant only by virtue of the democratic ideal, or the imperative to maximize the individuality-in-association of all humans. This ideal prescribes a social order that seeks to maximize the content of human sharing or communication. Implied in this formulation, I suggest, is a significant distinction between associations where communication is instrumental to other things, so that limits are placed upon it, and those where communication is the defining purpose, so that it may be maximized. I will call the former "consumption-regarding associations" and the latter "community-regarding associations."

The distinct purpose of consumption-regarding associations is to be instrumental to economic benefits, where such benefits are broadly defined to mean experiences that are primarily exclusive of human communication and, therefore, primarily inclusive of self, nature, or material things. To be sure, considerable communication occurs within consumption-regarding associations, especially among those engaged in directing them. But this communication is subservient to or limited by the instrumental purpose of the association and, therefore, is not designed to maximize the distinctive contribution of each to all. At the extreme, such communication becomes strictly the servant of exchange. That communication has this purpose is another way to formulate Dewey's criticism of earlier liberalism and of a "pecuniary culture" dominated by corporate, profit-seeking institutions. Were the social order reconstructed in accord with Dewey's prescriptions, the extent of human communication in consumption-regarding institutions would be vastly increased. As we have noted, those engaged in production and distribution would have a "share—imaginative, intellectual, and emotional—in directing the activities in which they physically participate" (1962, 131). Because economic institutions are presently dominant, and because the economic system would continue to demand a significant portion of most lives even in the best of reconstructions, Dewey insists that work must become an instrument of genuine culture, so that "the masses can freely share in a life enriched in imagination and esthetic enjoyment" (1962, 125). With industrial democracy and public supervision, economic interaction would become a significant occasion for cultivating distinctive individuals. By definition, however, the purpose of this interaction will remain in significant measure the production and distribution of things to be consumed, so that the individuality-in-association is instrumental to something else.

Community-regarding associations are those whose distinct purpose is nothing other than maximal human communication. Dewey suggests that this may be the case when association attends to "the values of intellectual, esthetic or companionship life" (1963a, 88). With the scientific community at its best as his model, Dewey suggests that associations defined by the common pursuit of ideas or aesthetic appreciation, or the sharing of human experience generally, permit an uncompromised appreciation of others' distinctiveness and engage human activity that is fully directed toward distinctive contributions to others. In educational, cultural, and "companionship" associations, we may say, the higher human capacities come into their own. It may be argued that nongovernmental political activity, activity whose purpose is public participation, also belongs among these capacities. Since the organization of the public is properly a matter of inquiry and education regarding public interests, political activity is, in the relevant respects, similar to, if not a part of, the life of ideas. Accordingly, public-interest associations provide a further occasion upon which individuality-in-association may be pursued for its own sake and, therefore, are also community-regarding.

For reasons already discussed, it is clear that consumption-regarding associations cannot be redefined as profit-seeking organizations, although any of the latter which might be present in Dewey's reconstructed social order would belong to this class. In addition, consumption-regarding associations are not limited to the equivalents of organizations that are, in contemporary America, part of the profit-seeking sector. On the contrary, some presently nonprofit organizations are included. Nonprofit health institutions, for instance, are principally instrumental to biological needs. Similarly, many social-service and welfare agencies, especially where their purpose is to alleviate poverty, are instrumental to economic benefits. In saying this, one no more deprecates these institutions than Dewey discounts the importance of the modern economy. If cooperative control of industry could make industrial organizations the locus of significant individuality-in-association, the same may well be true of health-delivery and welfare institutions. In any event, the intellectual, aesthetic, and political life is not possible in significant measure without sufficient economic activity to assure a "secure basis for an ordered expression of individual capacity and the satisfaction of the needs of man in non-economic directions" (1963a, 88).

Nonetheless, it is also true that Dewey's theory implies a teleological ordering of nongovernmental, democratic associations, such that consumption-regarding associations are subservient to community-regarding ones. Since maximal individuality-in-association is the telos of associational life, and since individuality-in-association is realized most fully when pursued for its own sake, consumption-regarding associations should be "servants of the development of the higher human capacities" (1963a, 32). If governmental associations are teleologically subservient to nongovernmental ones, it follows that the telos of the social order is to maximize community-regarding associations. Accordingly, the difference between earlier and reconstructed liberalism may be succinctly summarized: whereas the former makes economic or consumption-regarding associations teleologically prior, the latter makes them subservient to community-regarding ones. If that conclusion suggests again how fundamental is Dewey's critique of the contemporary social order, it also repeats his call for a public that recognizes itself and thereby moves out of "eclipse." For the reversal that is implied will require substantial public participation. It is fortunate, then, that voluntary public-interest associations are themselves community-regarding. Insofar as these associations are involved, the public process will itself illustrate the ideal to which it is directed. It is worth noting that such associations need not necessarily be participating in formal governmental procedures. Publics may sometimes at least try to care for their interests without appeal to official powers, as some aspects of the civil rights movement in the 1960s (e.g., its use of economic boycotts against nongovernmental institutions) illustrated. This is, perhaps, one advantage of Dewey's implication that a *different* public exists each time associational activity has important indirect consequences. If the interests in question are indeed public, however, the appeal to governmental power always remains as a possible recourse should the informal effort be ineffective, so that the activity in question is properly called political. These considerations suggest a further distinction within the class of community-regarding associations, namely, between public-interest associations and all others. The distinction is theoretically significant because the organization of the public has a distinct function in the associational order. We might now say that, in Dewey's view, the democratic telos of the social order will remain far more ideal than actual until sufficient new vitality is created in public-interest associations to bring the public out of eclipse.

In any event, we may also say that the class of community-regarding associations is, within Dewey's theory, the implied class of independent associations. Commonplace examples of American commercial institutions or their equivalents are all consumption-regarding, so that community-regarding associations constitute a significant class of nongovernmental, noncommercial organizations. If the benefits to which consumption-regarding associations are instrumental may indeed be called economic, it may be appropriate to say that all such associations are commercial, so that all noncommercial associations are community-regarding. In that case, Dewey's theory, like Friedman's but unlike Gewirth's, implies a threefold division of the social order into governmental, commercial, and independent associations. But the differences between Dewey and Friedman are as fundamental as Dewey's reconstruction of earlier liberalism. For Friedman, the commercial or profit-seeking sector is teleologically prior, so that independent associations are subservient to it and government, similarly subservient, is minimized. For Dewey, the commercial sector is teleologically subservient to community-regarding associations, so that government, similarly subservient, is (at least given the corporate conditions of contemporary America) greatly extended.

The understanding of the social order developed from Dewey's theory is schematically summarized in figure 4.

FIGURE 4
ASSOCIATIONS

Governmental	Nongovernmental		
	Consumption-regarding	Community-regarding	
		Nonpublic interest	Public interest

Critical Discussion

I have said that I selected Dewey's thought for review in this work as an illustration of reformed liberalism, where this is distinguished from both nineteenth- and twentieth-century established liberalism, illustrated respectively by Friedman and Gewirth. The distinction turns upon the presence or absence of a moral criterion in terms of which happiness or self-interest may be defined. Reformed liberalism includes such a criterion, so that theories of this type imply a distinction between genuine and putative self-interest. Established liberalism excludes such a criterion, so that theories of this type assert the preferential view of happiness. But I have not yet explicitly argued that Dewey's theory in fact illustrates reformed liberalism, so that the following question should now be addressed: Does Dewey's liberalism include a moral criterion in accord with which happiness or self-interest is defined?

Before we turn to this matter, however, a second question may be posed. I sought in chapter 4 to invalidate all established liberal theories by defending a formal condition for political theory that is contrary to the preferential view of happiness. This condition requires that political theory be informed by a comprehensive variable or principle for understanding and morally evaluating human activity, so that a moral criterion for happiness or self-interest is implied by that principle. If this succeeds in refuting established liberal theories, however, it also constitutes a formal condition for reformed liberalism, namely, that its criterion of self-interest should be derived from a comprehensive moral principle. Accordingly, the second question regarding Dewey's liberalism may be posed as follows: If it is reformed in character, is its criterion of self-interest implied by a comprehensive principle for understanding and evaluating human activity?

I will begin with the first of these two questions, whether Dewey's liberalism is reformed in the sense specified. Some of Dewey's statements might seem to imply a negative answer. Because he holds that human experience is contingent, he affirms "a plurality of changing, moving, individualized goods" and is emphatically opposed to moral thought which prescribes the pursuit of "fixed ends" (1957, 162, 165). He even says that ethical theory "has been singularly hypnotized by the notion that its business is to discover some final end or good or some ultimate and supreme law" (1957, 161) (a notion that belongs to unreconstructed liberalism). One might conclude that Dewey is committed to a relativism in human ends that is finally indistinguishable from the exercise of preference, so that self-interest is without any "fixed" or "supreme" criterion.

Whatever the merit of this reading, it asserts far more than its advocates are likely to intend. A commitment to the kind of relativism suggested implies not only a preferential view of happiness but also the preference theory of human choice. All choice, in other words, would be a matter of preference, so that there are no moral standards at all and no genuine thinking about proper human ends. Dewey's theory of human action and associations would be explicitly "value-free" and his empiricism explicitly independent of moral commitments.

This consequence makes it obvious that Dewey's intentions have been radically misunderstood. John E. Smith has written that the problem of bridging science and value "engaged Dewey from the beginning to the end of his career" (Smith, 138). Dewey's persistent attention to this problem is a display of his basic intent to complete the scientific revolution by making moral inquiry empirical in character. Dewey's entire purpose in reconstructing philosophy is fully to open human action and associations to *intelligent* evaluation. His repudiation of final goods, supreme laws, or fixed ends in no way intends to collapse the distinction between what *seems* good and what *is* good in human life. His attack upon traditional ethical theory has quite another target, namely, the notion that morals involve some "universal meaning that covers and dominates all particulars" (1957, 188) or "ready-made principles to be imposed upon particulars in order to determine their nature" (1957, 189). In other words, his denials, like his affirmation of the scientific method, are indeed meant to assert and protect human contingency and particularity against the "philosophic fallacy," but there is no question that he takes this to be a *moral* affirmation of human individuality.

For this reason, Dewey's disavowal of universals which disparage particularity does not prevent a general criterion that expresses his moral affirmations. This criterion is the democratic ideal, in accord with which action and association pursue "the all-around growth" of every member of society; he calls this the "only moral 'end'" (1957, 186, 177). "Growth" refers to maximal continuity or richness of experience through maximal inclusiveness. At the most general level, this ideal provides a measure by which particular choices or courses of action may be evaluated; some make a greater contribution to the growth of all than do their alternatives. Moreover, this general measure is an affirmation of human individuality, for it prescribes the maximal inclusiveness of human experiences in all their contingency and particularity.

If these considerations insist upon the obvious point that Dewey does not assert the preference theory of human choice, they also make clear that he does not advocate a preferential view of happiness. On the contrary, if the maximal growth of all is the "only moral 'end,'" the maximal growth of any one is the good for that individual. Happiness is maximal human individuality or inclusiveness of experience. One's self-interest is in no aspect solely a matter of preference but consists in the maximal inclusiveness of one's experience, and, with this criterion, Dewey provides the grounds to distinguish between genuine and putative self-interests in all their particularity. The established liberal view of happiness belongs to "earlier liberalism" or the "old individualism." Indeed, that view is another way to express that "economic individualism of motives and aims" which, in turn, "undoes the individual" (1962, 59) and to which the "new individualism" is meant to be an alternative. In short, Dewey's liberalism is not established but reformed.

Of course, just because this understanding of self-interest is a full affirmation of human contingency, it is also a full affirmation of human association. Maximal individuality is maximally constituted by association, so that we may say the same of happiness. To increase growth or inclusiveness of experience is nothing other than to increase the distinctiveness with which one acts in conjunction and connection with distinctive others. We have already seen that earlier and reconstructed liberalism differ not only with respect to individuals but also with respect to associations, and the one because of the other. Earlier liberalism, to which the established liberal view of happiness belongs, understands individuals to be creators but not creatures of their associations, so that "old individualism" takes associations to be instrumental to economic motives and aims, and seeks to maximize economic benefits. Reconstructed liberalism insists that contingent individuals are defined by their conditions and consequences, so that "new individualism" takes associations to be constitutive of individuality and seeks to maximize the content of human communication. The democratic ideal, which prescribes the happiness of all, calls for the maximal individuality-in-association of all.

We are now in a position to address the second of the two questions regarding Dewey's liberalism—whether its criterion of self-interest is implied by a comprehensive principle for understanding and evaluating human activity. At the least, we may say that a positive answer is plausible. For the principle in question is nothing other than individuality-in-association, or distinctiveness in connection with the distinctiveness of others. This is a comprehensive variable for understanding human activity, because all such activity is in some measure distinctiveness in connection with other distinctiveness. It is a comprehensive moral principle because maximal individuality-in-association for all is prescribed; the alternative choice that is superior in terms of this comprehensive variable is categorically required. So far from "value-free" theory is Dewey's intent that the democratic ideal is nothing other than the comprehensive variable for understanding human activity stated as its perfection. There are, to be sure, a number of matters to be clarified and defended prior to a judgment that Dewey's intent in this regard has been thoroughly fulfilled. Nonetheless, enough has been said to suggest that Dewey's theory presents a strong claim to the kind of comprehensiveness that liberalism must seek. Insofar as this claim can be vindicated, his reform liberalism is recommended in contrast to the established liberal tradition.

For all that, however, there is a pivotal issue that remains, namely, whether Dewey's theory is true. Does Dewey successfully defend or justify the comprehensive principle of individuality-in-association and thereby justify the theory of associations that it informs?

I mentioned earlier John E. Smith's comment that the bridge between science and value occupied Dewey's attention throughout his intellectual life. Because the comprehensive principle is moral in character, is the democratic ideal, the question may be posed in Smith's terms: Does Dewey successfully bridge science and value? His persistent return to this issue at least suggests that a difficulty of some moment is involved, and the apparent problem may be briefly stated: Scientific claims and moral claims seem to be logically distinct, such that one cannot derive the latter from the former. Given some situation of human activity, scientific observation and experimentation may be used to test claims regarding the particular facts of the case, the particular possibilities open, and the probable consequences of alternative courses of action. But that some specified alternative is valuable, in the sense that there is a reason for choosing it that is independent of the choice, seems to be a claim immune to the tests of methodical observation and experimentation. The question for Dewey, then, may be reformulated as follows: Although scientific inquiry is competent to evaluate the proposed *means* through which one might move from present conditions to desirable ends or consequences, is it not impotent to establish which ends or consequences are desirable?

This form of the question, Dewey replies, assumes a distinction between instrumentally and intrinsically good objects or states of affairs, such that some are "ends-in-themselves." To the contrary, he insists, means and ends form a continuum, such that every means is also an end, and vice versa. "Every condition that has to be brought into existence to serve as a means is, *in that connection*, an object of desire and an end-in-view, while the end attained is a means to future ends as well as a test of valuations previously made" (1939, 43). He appeals, in other words, to the inherently changing or processive character of human experience, which permits one to speak only of "ends-in-view," not of "ends-in-themselves," which is a vestigial concept from prescientific philosophy.

At the same time, Dewey recognizes that this appeal does not establish a distinction between better and worse "ends-in-view." *All* possible courses of human experience involve means which are ends and ends which are means, and the task of evaluation is to identify the desirable. "The objection always brought forth against the view set forth is that, according to it, valuation activities and judgments are involved in a hopeless *regressus ad infinitum*. If, so it is said, there is no end which is not in turn a means, foresight has no place at which it can stop, and no end-in-view can be formed except by the most arbitrary of acts—an act so arbitrary that it mocks the claim of being a genuine valuation-proposition" (1939, 45). In reply to this, Dewey appeals to his analysis of intelligence as problematic and, therefore, operational in character. "Valuation takes place only when there is something the matter; when there is some trouble to be done away with, some need, lack or privation to be made good, some conflict of tendencies to be resolved by means of changing existing conditions" (1939, 34; see also 45). The character of the problem defines appropriate or desirable ends-in-view for that situation or activity. "The difference in different desires and their correlative ends-in-view depends upon two things. The first is the adequacy with which inquiry into the lacks and conflicts of the existing situation has been carried on. The second is the adequacy of the inquiry into the likelihood that the particular ends-in-view will, if acted upon, actually fill the existing need" (1939, 35). But Dewey's solution remains unconvincing. Problems themselves cannot be defined independently of evaluation, as though the character of a particular problem might set the terms through which good and bad actions are distinguished. Situations are wanting or problematic in a moral sense only because they fall short of a moral ideal; one must have a prior understanding of desirable ends-in-view in order to know that there is "some trouble to be made good." Accordingly, I take John E. Smith's conclusion to be correct: Dewey "did not solve the problem of how to determine ultimate ends" (Smith, 143).

Of course, it does not follow from Dewey's failure that the problem is unresolvable. The possibility is left open that a sound argument might be formulated to fulfill his purpose. But if his persistent return to the problem suggests the presence of a difficulty, it also indicates that something utterly fundamental is at stake. Through pursuing the implications of this problem in Dewey's thought, I now propose to confirm his failure to solve that problem by showing that, in his thought, a resolution is impossible.

Fundamental issues are involved because the problem of science and value results from Dewey's commitment to empirical pragmatism. The democratic ideal must be verifiable by the scientific method because his commitment to each is a way to express his fundamental philosophical position. All intelligence is a practical intervention between contingent conditions and consequences. Thus, Dewey reasons, the method of intelligence must be empirical or scientific and its purpose can only be maximal growth of experience for all, or maximal democracy. Were he to admit that an unbridgeable chasm yawns between science and value, he would be forced to conclude that something is fundamentally amiss with his reconstruction in philosophy. Moreover, behind this understanding of philosophy lies Dewey's metaphysics of universal process, which he takes to be inseparable from the scientific revolution. Intelligence is a practical intervention of the sort described because all things are contingencies-in-association. In Dewey's thought, then, the possibility of bridging science and value depends upon two prior assertions, the second of which also logically depends upon the first:

(1) All things are contingencies-in-association.
(2) Intelligence as such is practical in the empirical sense.

We may pose the question of Dewey's justification for his comprehensive principle by asking whether these two prior claims can be verified.

Let us begin with the second: intelligence as such is practical in the empirical sense. It follows directly that Dewey's method of verifying this assertion is given by the assertion itself (the assertion itself can only be practically verified). Like all other assertions, it is an empirical hypothesis to be tested. "Notions, theories, systems, no matter how elaborate or self-consistent they are, must be regarded as hypotheses" (1957, 145). Dewey's understanding of intelligence, like all other hypotheses, is verified if it "works." "The hypothesis that works is the true one; and truth is an abstract noun applied to the collection of cases, actual, foreseen and desired, that receive confirmation in their works and consequences" (1957, 156–57). But now a profound circularity in Dewey's enterprise becomes apparent. The test of whether a hypothesis works when it is acted upon is finally defined in terms of human growth or continuity in experience—by the ideal of democracy—but we have just seen that the affirmation of this ideal depends upon the assertion to be tested, that intelligence is practical. This profound circularity is also logically vicious. For testing by consequences requires that the basis or criterion of judgment be logically independent of the truth or falsity of the assertion to be tested. This is the meaning of empirical testing. Were the grounds for verification logically dependent upon the truth or falsity of the assertion in question, this assertion would not be an empirical hypothesis. It would be true or false analytically, by definition, so that verification or falsification need not wait upon a test of consequences. In Dewey's empirical pragmatism, however, the ideal of democracy logically depends upon the truth of "all intelligence is practical." This assertion does not permit the empirical test that it requires. It is internally incoherent and, accordingly, cannot be true. Since Dewey's affirmation of the democratic ideal logically depends upon this assertion, it follows that the democratic ideal cannot be justified in Dewey's thought.

There is another way to reach the same conclusion. If "all intelligence is practical" were true, not only that assertion itself but also the democratic ideal must be verifiable by consequences. In other words, "all human action ought to pursue the maximal growth of all individuals" is also an empirical hypothesis which is tested by whether it "works." But clearly the test of that hypothesis has no logically independent criterion, since the ideal of democracy is itself the criterion for empirical tests. The validity of the democratic ideal has to be presupposed in order to have a pragmatic test for the hypothesis of the democratic ideal. One arrives again at the conclusion that the democratic ideal cannot be justified by empirical pragmatism. Because empirical pragmatism requires the democratic ideal in order to test practical hypothesis, it follows that "all intelligence is practical" is internally incoherent. In his attempt to be empirically pragmatic, Dewey seeks to drive even the affirmation of empirical pragmatism into a pragmatic test; but, with this, the entire enterprise is lost at sea.

The entire enterprise is nothing other than the theory of associations informed by the democratic ideal, and, if the critique offered above is sound, Dewey's attempt to test his theory pragmatically must be a failure. That attempt rests upon the claim that reconstructed liberalism resolves the basic problems within contemporary community life. Dewey traces these problems to the duality between the physical and the moral, especially in the sense that earlier liberalism as the dominant influence on moral thought is based upon the notion of separate or isolated individuals. He then details how acting upon his theory of associations would overcome contemporay stresses and strains. But this argument will not long withstand examination. As I noted in the earlier discussion of science and value, the claim that certain contemporary conditions constitute moral problems is an assertion already informed by a moral ideal. It is equivalent to the claim that these conditions ought not to exist, or, at least, ought to be changed. The associational expressions of a disparity between the physical and the distinctively human are problematic only if one has already assumed that the democratic ideal identifies the good. Dewey has no grounds from which to criticize earlier liberalism, with all of its consequences in contemporary corporate society, save that these consequences are antidemocratic. Thus, the claim that this ideal and the theory informed by it are justified because action based upon it resolves the problems is again viciously circular. The conclusion is inescapable that Dewey's empirical pragmatism is fundamentally incoherent and, therefore, cannot be true.

If this line of thought shows that the democratic ideal cannot be scientifically or empirically verified, attention must be turned to the first of the two assertions upon which Dewey's theory of associations depends: All things are contingencies-in-association. Dewey's embrace of empirical pragmatism is, he thinks, entailed by this metaphysics. If empirical pragmatism cannot be true, does it follow that this metaphysics is also unfounded? Clearly, the answer is positive if Dewey's understanding is correct, if the metaphysics implies the method. If X cannot be true, then nothing which entails X can be true. This can be seen in another way: If the metaphysics entails radical empiricism, then universal contingency-in-association can be verified only by the empirical test of consequences. But the criterion of this test—the ideal of democracy—would depend upon the metaphysics. Again a supposed hypothesis would require but not permit a logically independent basis for its empirical test. Thus, the metaphysics could not be true.

Whether Dewey's metaphysics does entail empirical empiricism depends upon how the notion of universal contingency-in-association is understood. In order for the entailment to hold, this universal character of existence must itself be contingent, in the sense that existence might have had some other universal character but in fact has this one. It follows that there is no alternative to an empirical test of this metaphysical claim. It is my judgment that this is the sense in which Dewey advanced metaphysical assertions. By my reading, he believed metaphysical traits to be contingent because he thought this the only alternative to the classical philosophy in which eternal or fixed universals "dominated" contingent particulars and the changeable was taken to be a lesser form of reality. It is for this reason that his own religious sensibilities could find expression only in "a common faith" which excluded theistic belief (see 1934). Theism for Dewey asserts another form of fixed being which does not permit the full affirmation of contingency-in-association. If this reading is correct, it is simply an expression of what is clearly the most persuasive evidence that Dewey held even metaphysical traits to be contingent, the evidence furnished by his thorough conviction that his metaphysics implied empirical pragmatism.

But it is not immediately evident that Dewey's understanding of universal contingency-in-association is the only possible one. One might assert that the metaphysical traits of contingency-in-association are themselves necessary in the sense that all possible realities must exhibit them. If this metaphysical understanding is correct, the contingent particularity of all realities will still be affirmed but empirical pragmatism does not follow. It remains to say, then, that the criticism of Dewey's pragmatism offered here does not necessarily repudiate the ideal of democracy. All that has been shown is that this ideal cannot be justified *if* empirical pragmatism is affirmed. But it remains open whether an alternative understanding of universal process may permit a justification of Dewey's theory of associations.

Six

Toward a Constructive Political Theory

In this chapter I will pursue the possibility that an alternative understanding of universal contingency-in-association may permit a coherent affirmation of Dewey's theory of associations. The discussion will begin by clarifying the alternative understanding of metaphysics. It will then argue that human activity entails an evaluative variable that is metaphysical. Subsequently, I will seek to refine the notion of contingency-in-association in order to show that it can be understood as an evaluative variable in terms of which something very like Dewey's theory of associations might be given an appropriate justification.

In this discussion, I am deeply indebted to the general metaphysical position that has come to be known as "process philosophy." Dewey's metaphysics might itself be called one of universal process. Hence, there is a legitimate sense in which the term suggests a more general philosophical movement than that to which I refer. More specifically, it designates the metaphysical perspective of Alfred North Whitehead and those who take their philosophical bearings from him. Among the latter, the most important resource is the thought of Charles Hartshorne, who creatively appropriated Whitehead's metaphysics in directions that permit greater logical rigor. If there is merit to the suggestion that process philosophy in this sense provides a coherent metaphysical context for Dewey's theory of association, the gain is as much to this process tradition as to Dewey. Neither Whitehead nor Hartshorne—nor any of those who take their bearings from their thought—have written a more or less comprehensive political theory, although there have been recent efforts to pursue more fully the political implications of the perspective (see Cobb; Cobb and Schroeder; Hall; Ogden, 1979). Success in the appropriation which this chapter seeks to forward would suggest that Dewey's politics provides an immensely valuable resource for that pursuit.

Metaphysics

For the present purposes, the important differentia of process philosophy in the Whiteheadian sense is the conviction that metaphysical characteristics are themselves necessary rather than contingent. We have seen that Dewey's metaphysics is consistent with his adherence to empirical pragmatism only if contingency-in-association is understood to be a contingent trait. When Dewey says that metaphysics is "a statement of the generic traits manifested by existence of all kinds without regard to their differentiation into physical and mental" (1958, 412), empirical pragmatism follows only if these generic traits might have been other than they are. Process philosophy in the specific sense informing this chapter holds that the metaphysical traits could not be other than they are and, therefore, are necessary. Although this constitutes a fundamental break with empirical pragmatism, it does not follow that the verification of metaphysical claims makes no appeal to experience. Because metaphysical traits necessarily characterize all existence, they must be present in any and all experienced realities. Whitehead says that metaphysical claims must be applicable; that is, there must be some possible experience to which one may direct attention and in which the putative metaphysical trait is exhibited. Metaphysical claims, he continues, must also be adequate; that is, there can be no possible experience which fails to exhibit the trait in question (see Whitehead 1978, 3–4). In the absence of adequacy, applicable claims are nonmetaphysical. Of course, a claim that is genuinely adequate is necessarily applicable, indeed is applicable to any possible experienced reality. But applicability is an important part of the metaphysical test because it protects against conceptual vagueness. By virtue of its subject matter, metaphysical discussion is ever threatened by putative concepts which in their high generality may seem to say something but are in truth applicable to no possible experience. Such concepts are hopelessly vague and, in that sense, meaningless. In any event, it is the demand for adequacy that makes Whitehead's metaphysical appeal to experience different than Dewey's; the former is not, if I may put it so, an empirical appeal to experience. For metaphysical claims are adequate by virtue of their applicability to all possible realities in the strictest sense, to all conceivable realities. Metaphysical traits are necessary in that they "bear within themselves their own warrant of universality throughout all experience" (Whitehead 1978, 4). From this it follows that verification does not wait upon a test of consequences. Metaphysical traits are shown to be applicable and adequate by demonstrating that reality in which they are absent is inconceivable.

Charles Hartshorne presents the same meaning of "metaphysical" when he speaks of the difference between local and cosmic (non-metaphysical and metaphysical) variables (Hartshorne 1937, 111–25). Hartshorne uses the term "variable" as I did in the fourth chapter of this work—to identify a trait or characteristic in terms of which two or more realities can be compared. Local variables, says Hartshorne, are those which are or might be exemplified in some but not all conceivable realities, so that only some realities can be compared in terms of them. Self-consciousness is such a local variable. Differing instances of human activity can be compared according to, say, the clarity and breadth of their respective exemplifications of self-consciousness—but not so, differing instances of plant life. Life itself may be a variable in terms of which various exemplifications of plant life can be compared, and plant life as such may be compared to human life. Thus, life may be called a wider variable than self-consciousness, in that the latter is a specification or "value" of the former. But life remains a local variable, because it does not provide the terms within which to compare differing instances of inorganic existence. In contrast, cosmic or metaphysical variables are those of which every conceivable reality is an instance, such that all possible realities may be compared in terms of them. Cosmic variables define what it means to be a possible reality in the most general sense; they define possibility as such. As in Whitehead, therefore, so in Hartshorne, "metaphysical" refers to necessary rather than contingent traits of existence. As exhibited in all conceivable realities, these traits could not conceivably be different.

I argued in chapter 4 that self-conscious activity entails a comprehensive comparative variable in terms of which all alternatives for human choice may be understood, and that this variable is a comprehensive moral principle in terms of which all alternatives for human choice may be evaluated. In pursuit of the possibility that the process understanding of metaphysics provides a coherent perspective within which to appropriate Dewey's theory of associations, I now wish to argue that this comprehensive moral principle must be a specification to human activity of a comprehensive evaluative variable that is metaphysical. I will argue that understanding and evaluating human activity entails a comprehensive cosmic variable for understanding and evaluating reality as such.

The relevance of this argument to the discussion of Dewey should be indicated. It was one of the conclusions of chapter 5 that Dewey asserts a comprehensive variable and principle in terms of which human activities may be compared—the variable of individuality-in-association and the principle of maximal individuality-in-association. It is also true that

Dewey understands individuality-in-association to be, in one respect, a specification of generic traits of existence. All realities are contingencies-in-association and human activity is simply the specifically intelligent form of this universal characteristic. But the specification thereby suggested is in one respect only, for contingency-in-association is not, for Dewey, as individuality-in-association is, an evaluative principle. As generic, the trait has no evaluative status. Value is for Dewey something realized in or characterizing human experience alone, so that "good" is only growth in human experience. Nonhuman realities may contribute to value or to good by virtue of the fact that human experience is related to them; the nonhuman environment is both supportive and threatening to human growth, and in that derivative sense it might also be called good or bad. But the sense is strictly derivative. Value in its primary sense refers to human experience; growth is the only moral end. Accordingly, contingency-in-interaction is evaluative solely in its peculiarly human specification. This understanding of value is, I suggest, another reflection of Dewey's empirical pragmatism. Because all statements are tested practically, good and bad must be defined in terms of human experience. If nonhuman reality could be good-in-itself, a statement to this effect could not be practically tested. It follows that the circularity of empirical pragmatism can also be revealed by showing that an evaluation of human experience entails a metaphysical evaluation, or that, as evaluative, the comprehensive variable for human activity must be a specification of a variable that is cosmic.

An argument to this effect may be approached by reformulating Dewey's position in Hartshorne's terms. Because value is peculiarly human, Dewey holds that the variable by which human alternatives are evaluated is local to human existence. It should be clear that there is a trivial sense in which this assertion is true. The variable for evaluating human choice alternatives is local to human existence because it need be no wider than the possible instances of human experience. Similarly, if one holds that human existence alone enjoys moral freedom (if only humans have the capacity to choose between categorically required and categorically proscribed alternatives) then it follows that the comprehensive moral principle is local to human existence. As we have seen, however, Dewey also implies that the variable for evaluating human activity is local to human existence in a nontrivial sense, namely, that only human experiences or choice alternatives admit of being good or bad, better or worse. Although individuality-in-association is, for purposes of understanding, a specification of the wider trait, contingency-in-association, the latter has no evaluative character. Consequently the comprehensive moral principle is local in a nontrivial sense.

The inconsistency in this position may be generally suggested. For Dewey, the wider variable, contingency-in-association, is one in terms of which instances of human existence may be compared to instances of nonhuman existence, and one consequence of this comparison is that the former may be good or bad while the latter are neither good nor bad. But this consequence seems to require that the wider variable be evaluative.

This conclusion may be confirmed by examining Dewey's implied claim that nonhuman realities might contribute to the value of human experience. Clearly, all human activity includes relations to nonhuman realities, e.g., to the subhuman world in some of its patterns, including especially the human body but also the world of human artifacts. If these human activities are evaluated, then an evaluation of their nonhuman constituents is included. Thus, for instance, the difference between seeing a sunset and seeing a stone involves an evaluation of the sunset and the stone as actual or possible constituents of human experience. On a more generous scale, the choice between preserving the Alaskan wilderness or opening the land to energy exploration turns in part upon an evaluative comparison of the wilderness and the possible material benefits of the energy resources. But an evaluation of these nonhuman constituents cannot be included unless the variable of which they are instances is evaluative. If, for example, contingency-in-association is the trait in terms of which *all* constituents of human activity are comparable, then this variable must be evaluative, such that greater is always better than lesser contingency-in-association. If the moral principle is nontrivially local, nonhuman realities cannot be instances of it and, therefore, cannot be evaluated. There would be no evaluative difference between human sight of a sunset and human sight of a stone, since the evaluation must abstract from the sunset and the stone. Thus, it is inconsistent for Dewey to imply that the better and worse are nontrivially local to human experience *and* that nonhuman realities contribute to value. Of course, he is committed to the latter if human individuality-in-association is to be a comprehensive moral principle, one by which all aspects of human choice alternatives are compared. Consequently, this moral principle must be a specification of a wider variable in terms of which all nonhuman realities constitutive of human alternatives may also be evaluated. The comprehensive moral principle must be a specification of a wider evaluative variable because, as constituents of human alternatives, nonhuman realities become morally relevant. The comprehensive moral principle cannot be nontrivially local to human experience, and, since this position is implied by Dewey's empirical pragmatism, the latter is again seen to be incoherent.

This line of thought in criticism of Dewey may be extended to show that the widest evaluative variable is metaphysical. In order for human activity to be comprehensively evaluated, the moral principle must be a specification of a wider variable of which all nonhuman constituents of human activity are also instances. The issue that remains is whether this wider variable may still be local rather than cosmic in character. Since local variables are those of which some conceivable realities are not instances, the wider variable could still be local only if some conceivable realities cannot be constituents of human choice alternatives. Clearly, there are some conceivable realities which one can safely say will never be experienced as actual, such as realities in some distant future or in some distant galaxy. But this is beside the point. Because they are conceivable realities, they do or can become constituents of human alternatives *as conceivable*; and, therefore, as conceivable they must exemplify characteristics in terms of which they can be evaluated. In short, the wider evaluative variable must be one exhibited by all conceivable realities. But precisely this is the definition of a cosmic or metaphysical variable. Accordingly, all possible realities may be evaluated as better or worse, and value must be understood as a characteristic inscribed, as it were, in the foundations of the universe. If contingency-in-association is a metaphysical trait (in the Whitehead-Hartshorne, not Dewey, sense), then realities are better insofar as they are greater, and worse insofar as they are less, in terms of this variable. Further, the comprehensive moral principle is the specification of this variable to human activity, which means that the human choice alternative (or class of alternatives) which maximizes contingency-in-association is categorically required.

This argument has proceeded on the grounds that all conceivable realities might be constituents of human choice alternatives, so that the comprehensive moral principle is a specification of a metaphysical variable. It then follows that a metaphysical evaluation is implied by any self-conscious activity, because any human self-understanding implies a comprehensive moral principle. No instance of human activity is understood without including in some measure an evaluation of all conceivable reality. The argument, therefore, may be repeated on this basis. Self-consciousness, as I noted in chapter 4, is the capacity to know oneself. By the same token, it is a capacity to know in some measure all others that one is not. Knowing oneself is simultaneously a knowing of all possible others as somehow different than oneself. But this means that self-knowledge involves a comparison of the self with all other conceivable realities. The sense in which this comparison is effected may be highly general, in that most other things are known to be simply other instances of a comparative variable of which the self is this particular instance. Nonetheless, even this most general comparison requires a variable of which all conceivable realities are instances. The correct understanding of alternatives for choice involves not only the comparison of each with the others but also a comparison of those alternatives with all conceivable realities that the self cannot be or become. Because the variable by which human alternatives are understood is evaluative, so too is the cosmic variable by which choice alternatives are compared to all other possible realities, since cosmic comparison is involved in every self-understanding. Every instance of human activity entails a metaphysical evaluation.

Consequently, we may say that the cosmic evaluative variable is the necessary and sufficient evaluative condition for identifying moral or categorically required choices. That it is necessary is simply another way of saying that the comprehensive moral principle *must* be a specification of a cosmic evaluation. That it is sufficient follows from the fact that its moral specification is comprehensive; to show that one alternative (or class of alternatives) is superior in terms of the cosmic evaluative variable is to show that this alternative is categorically required. It may also be said that the verification or justification of moral claims logically depends upon a metaphysical principle, in that this principle is the necessary and sufficient evaluative condition for such verification. This conclusion clarifies, and thereby limits, the enduring truth that is embodied in the well-known assertion that facts do not imply values, or "is" does not entail "ought." Because ethical justification depends upon a cosmic principle, no moral claim can be derived solely from the local characteristics or features of realities. The fact that certain actual or possible realities exhibit certain local characteristics rather than others never entails any moral conclusions. It is for this reason that Dewey's inclusive commitment to empiricism precludes a justification for his democratic ideal. The enduring truth in the difference between "is" and "ought" is that science cannot build a bridge to value. It does not follow, however, that "ought" can *never* be derived from "is," so that moral claims are always logically independent of statements about reality. Because moral claims depend upon a metaphysical variable, a metaphysical statement about reality, as specified to human activity, does imply a moral claim. The metaphysical variable *is* an evaluative principle.

It should also be said explicitly that the metaphysically evaluative variable must be the only metaphysical variable; it must be metaphysically comprehensive, thereby defining conceivable reality as such. For it is reality as such which, as conceivable, enters into all human self-understandings. The necessary and sufficient evaluative condition for the justification of ethical claims is nothing other than a variable or principle in accord with which all of reality may be comprehensively understood and evaluated. This is not to deny that the comprehensive metaphysical character may be analyzed in terms of its aspects, so that one might speak, as Hartshorne does, of several cosmic variables (1937, 111–25). One might hold that contingency, freedom, and association are all metaphysical traits. But these traits, if genuinely metaphysical, must all entail each other, so that to name any one is implicitly to name them all, and thereby to name the comprehensive metaphysical principle.

Finally, it is worth noting that this argument sets the terms for a discussion of the relation between religion and morality. There are many aspects of that relation, and a great deal depends upon what is meant by the term "religion." From at least one meaning thereof, however, we may conclude that the relation between religion and morality is fundamental to both. I refer to the definition of "religion" found in the following statements of Clifford Geertz:

> Never merely metaphysics, religion is never merely ethics either. The source of its moral vitality is conceived to lie in the fidelity with which it expresses the fundamental nature of reality. The powerfully coercive "ought" is felt to grow out of a comprehensive factual "is" and in such a way religion grounds the most specific requirements of human action in the most general contexts of human existence. (Geertz, 126)
>
> Sacred symbols thus relate an ontology and a cosmology to an aesthetics and a morality: their power comes from their presumed ability to identify fact with value at the most fundamental level, to give what is otherwise merely actual, a comprehensive normative import. (127)

Geertz goes on to claim that "the tendency to synthesize world view and ethos at some level, if it is not logically necessary, is at least empirically coercive; if it is not philosophically justified, it is a least pragmatically universal" (127). The argument I have presented has sought to establish that this tendency *is* philosophically justified because it is logically necessary. Because all human activity entails a comprehensive metaphysical variable that is also evaluative, fact and value are identified at the most fundamental level. Given Geertz's definition, we may say that the necessary and sufficient evaluative condition for identifying categorically required choices is a religious principle.

Morality

If we grant that moral justification depends upon a metaphysical principle, the argument for that conclusion has not yet justified any definite ethical claims. In order to identify which human alternatives ought to be chosen, one must know not only that a metaphysical variable is required but also what its character is. In what do metaphysically better and worse consist? In the remainder of this chapter, I will propose an answer to that question and pursue the theory of associations implied by that answer. But I can do no more than suggest a constructive formulation. Something approaching a comprehensive treatment of the matter would be more or less a complete metaphysics and political theory. The attempt here is to outline an argument through which Dewey's theory of associations might be given an appropriate metaphysical backing.

In seeking the character of the comprehensive cosmic principle, it is well to reiterate that metaphysical statements should be, as Whitehead has it, both applicable and adequate. They must find clear exemplification in some experienced reality and cannot be absent in any conceivable reality. The one experienced reality which has been most fully discussed in this work is that of human activity itself, experienced self-consciously, and applicability might be assured through beginning with a return to this reality. I argued in chapter 4 that human activity is in part self-determined, is a choice among real alternatives. Self-consciousness cannot be completely caused by others. At the same time, human activity is in part other-determined. Causes beyond the self define and thereby limit the alternatives among which any given human activity is a choice, because there must be something of which the self is conscious. Partial self-determination means that any given human activity is contingent; it might have been different. Partial other-determination means that any given human activity is associated; it is constituted by relations to others, and the others with which activity is associated are not solely its prior causes but also the subsequent others of which the activity will be a cause. One may say, with Dewey, that human activity is contingency-in-association. If self-consciousness is taken as the distinctively human characteristic, then human activity is self-conscious contingency-in-association. Since this conclusion means that Dewey's generic traits are applicable to human activity, the metaphysical question is whether they are adequate. Can one conceive of a reality in which contingency-in-association is absent?

An appropriate treatment of that question would take this work far beyond its present scope and, in any case, require far more than my competence allows. With respect to that more thorough treatment, I can only assert my conviction that Whitehead and Hartshorne have developed in more or less complete fashion a persuasive case for an affirmative answer. My purpose here is simply to outline considerations which serve to make that affirmative answer initially plausible. Given that contingency-in-association means partial self-determination, a reality which does not exemplify this trait must be either completely self-determined or completely other-determined. Since the distinctions between these three alternatives are based upon the exhaustive distinctions between all, some, and none (all = completely self-determined; some = partially self-determined; none = completely other-determined), the three alternatives exhaust the logical possibilities. The question is whether a reality which is completely self-determined or completely other-determined is conceivable.

The assertion that some reality or realities are completely self-determined has found philosophical expression in some forms of theism, according to which the divine is completely self-sufficient, and some extreme forms of solipsism, according to which human existence is completely self-created. It is also implied in what Whitehead calls the doctrine of "simple location" that underlies Newtonian physics, according to which "each bit of matter" is "fully describable apart from any reference to any other portion of matter" and "without any reference to past or future" (Whitehead 1961, 156; see also 1925, 50f., 57f.). None of these three claims finds wide adherence in contemporary philosophy, and, I suggest, that is because complete self-determination is impossible. Suppose, first, that a reality is said to be completely determined by choice, as in extreme solipsism. I have argued previously that a human self which is in no respect other-determined would have nothing of which to be conscious; similarly, a reality which is completely self-chosen would have nothing to choose among. Self-determination without some limitation upon or definition of the alternatives among which the self chooses is a completely negative expression—a determination without any definition of what is being determined—and is, therefore, indistinguishable from nothing. A completely self-chosen reality could not be necessarily different than anything else, since necessary difference is a nonchosen limitation. But a reality which is not necessarily different from anything else is completely indeterminate, and complete indeterminacy is indistinguishable from nothing.

The same conclusion may be reached if we suppose, second, that a reality is said to be completely self-determined by nature. Something like this is a traditional theistic claim regarding divine self-sufficiency; in no respect could the divine conceivably be other than it is, so that it is completely self-determined by its own necessity. Justice to this tradition and to the issues involved demands a considerably detailed discussion, although one who wishes to defend this theistic concept should attend to the comprehensive arguments that Charles Hartshorne has advanced against it (see especially Hartshorne 1962; 1970). In any event, I suggest that a completely necessary reality is also indistinguishable from nothing. If it is necessary in all respects, it could not imply even the positive possibility of some other reality, because any positive implication would be an aspect of its necessity. A completely necessary reality cannot be distinguished (from anything) or, what is the same, is indistinguishable from nothing. Whether by choice or by nature, I suggest, complete self-determination is impossible.

The assertion that some reality or realities is completely other-determined has been advanced in many forms. Some of these are theistic, according to which the divine pre-determines everything that happens; others are naturalistic, according to which events are completely the product of prior causes by way of changeless "natural laws." The two are not mutually exclusive; some have held that the divine determines events completely by imposing natural laws. Indeed, Whitehead argues that the metaphysics behind Newtonian philosophy combines divine imposition of natural law with the doctrine of simple location (see 1961, 113). In any case, I suggest that Charles Hartshorne has advanced a decisive argument against the notion of complete other-determination. "Causal explanation," says Hartshorne, "is incurably pluralistic: on the basis of many past events, it has to explain a single present event. . . . It is then simple logic that something is missed by the causal account. . . . There can be no logic for such a derivation. The step [that is missed] is . . . a free creation" (Hartshorne 1970, 2). The point is that no one of the causes can determine the unity or singularity of the activity in question; to do so, a given cause would have *to effect* the relation *of its effect* with others. Were that possible, the determination of a given cause would be greater than its determination, which is impossible. Nor is it helpful to add that a pluralism of past events explains a single present event through the imposition of natural law. For the natural law then becomes an additional cause, and its relation to the many past causes remains unexplained. Just as self-consciousness transcends the other-determination of human action, so the unity of any given reality transcends the multiplicity of prior causes. All realities are in some measure self-determined, and the distinctive character of human activity is that unification there becomes, or is, self-conscious.

If both complete self-determination and complete other-determination are impossible, all realities must be partially self-determined (and, therefore, partially other-determined); they must be contingencies-in-association. If the argument at the beginning of this chapter is sound, so that human activity entails a cosmic or metaphysical variable, the argument for Dewey's metaphysical trait may be reformulated in terms of the implications of human activity. The local variable of which all human choices are instances must constitute a range of "values" within, or a specification of, the metaphysical variable in accord with which all realities are understood and evaluated. Of what variable other than contingency-in-association could self-conscious contingency-in-association be a specification? As I have noted, the only logical alternatives are complete self-determination or complete other-determination. But partial self-determination (e.g., human activity) is not a specification or value of either complete self-determination or complete other-determination. Freedom within limits is not a specification of freedom without limits or of complete necessity; indeed, the latter two are not variables at all. Accordingly, the character of reality as such must be contingency-in-association.

I suggest, then, that there are at least initial reasons to appropriate Dewey's generic trait, such that contingency-in-association is metaphysical. Both Whitehead and Hartshorne affirm this in their own terms. Each defines a reality as an "actual occasion" or "concrete event" or "unit or process" which is partially other-determined by prior causes to which it is related and partially self-determined in its unification of those relations. In their human forms, these units of process might be called either experiences or activities, the former emphasizing the fact that they are other-determined and the latter that they are self-determined. Whitehead and Hartshorne explicitly add what is implicit in Dewey's formulation, that each event will also become a cause of subsequent events, so that this inevitability is a constitutive relation to the future. Each unit of process, as Whitehead puts it, "arises as an effect facing its past and ends as a cause facing its future" (Whitehead 1961, 194). The definition of all possible realities is given in Whitehead's principle of creativity: "the many become one and are increased by one" (Whitehead 1978, 21).

If contingency-in-association, so understood, is, at least when all its implications are taken into account, the comprehensive metaphysical variable in terms of which all reality is properly understood and evaluated, this variable will serve as the necessary and sufficient condition for evaluative claims only if it may be so formulated as to admit of greater and lesser exhibitions or instances; better and worse require superior and inferior in some sense. Such a formulation is implied in

Whitehead's principle of creativity. Because realities are the many become one, they are greater or less in their unity-in-diversity, in the extent of diversity and the extent of unification. All realities include relationships to others, but the many to which each is related may be more or less complex as opposed to more or less simple; all realities are unifications, but the unification may be more or less harmonious as opposed to more or less dissonant. The variable in question is aesthetic in character and realities are superior and inferior in their measure of both unity and diversity, or harmony by way of complexity-in-contrast. Both Whitehead and Hartshorne call this variable "beauty" (for Whitehead's treatment, see especially 1961, 252–65; for Hartshorne's treatment, see especially 1970, 303–21).

If this formulation seems vague, it should be noted that the applicability of "unity-in-diversity" is established by any human experience, wherein relationships to many other realities are composed into just that singular event, and the notion of greater and lesser unity-in-diversity may be exhibited by comparing two such experiences, one relatively complex and the other relatively simple, one relatively harmonious and the other relatively dissonant. If the formulation seems highly general, it should be noted that generality of the highest order is the only possible answer to a question regarding all conceivable realities. Unity expresses the self-determination and diversity expresses the other-determination of reality as such, and unity-in-diversity serves as an appropriation within process metaphysics of Dewey's trait, contingency-in-association. Either formulation may be used to indicate the comprehensive metaphysical variable, which as a comprehensive principle of evaluation is maximal unity-in-diversity or maximal contingency-in-association. "The teleology of the universe" as Whitehead puts it, "is directed to the production of beauty" (Whitehead 1961, 265).

It follows from what has been said that the measure of beauty possible in any given concrete event depends upon the character of the many which are its causes. Unity-in-diversity is the many become one. Insofar as the many is both more diverse and more ordered or associated—is, in a word, more complex—the concrete event in question enjoys greater possibilities for good, and this is simply another expression of the aesthetic character of reality. "The universe," says Whitehead, "achieves its values by reason of its coordination into societies of societies and into societies of societies of societies," i.e., into enduring associations of diversity or complex causal relations (Whitehead 1961, 206). The especially rich possibilities of beauty in human experience result from the massive complexity of which it is an effect, including especially the complexity of the human body. What this causal power permits is, of course, self-conscious freedom, as opposed to the more limited self-determination of subhuman existence. In this sense other-determination and self-determination are positively correlated; greater complexity in the former means greater scope for the latter, and the especially rich inheritance of human existence yields the special privileges of human freedom.

The discussion is now in a position to return to the comprehensive moral principle and, through it, to move toward political theory. Moral evaluations, as we have seen, are specifications of the comprehensive metaphysical evaluation to situations of human choice—or, in the terms borrowed from Dewey, of maximal contingency-in-association to situations of individuality-in-association. The reintroduction of "individuality," however, requires some attention. In common usage, including that of Dewey, "human individual" is not equivalent to a human concrete event, at least as this latter term has been employed in the preceding paragraphs. "Human individual" commonly means a person, whose life is constituted by the sequence or "stream" of experience that extends from birth to death. Similarly, Hartshorne uses "individual" and Whitehead uses the term "personal society" to indicate a temporal sequence of events or experiences, so ordered that no two are contemporary and so related that the efficaciousness of these events is greater within the sequence than upon the rest of the world. The individual is distinguished from the rest of the world by a peculiar and, therefore, defining characteristic or set of characteristics which persists throughout members of the sequence by virtue of this causal coordination. I will reserve "individual" to mean a specifically human sequence of events, distinguished by those peculiar traits that persist from birth to death and that make the person this individual and not something else. The term "activity" will be used to indicate one of those concrete human events included within the life of an individual. Thus "activity-in-association" is a more precise term for the specifically human form of contingency-in-association or unity-in-diversity.

In their primary reference, then, moral evaluations refer to activities-in-association, and it follows from the metaphysical principle that, for any given activity, the alternative which is superior in terms of unity-in-diversity is categorically required. The comprehensive moral principle may be formulated: so act as to maximize unity-in-diversity. There is, however, an apparent ambiguity in this formulation which should be clarified. Since the many become one and are increased by one, each action is a unity-in-diversity and will be a cause of subsequent unities-in-diversity. The maximal unity-in-diversity prescribed might be that of the activity in question or that of all relevant realities, including those in the future. Is the agent categorically required to maximize the beauty of present activity or to pursue maximal beauty in reality as such?

Clearly, the latter is implied. Because the comprehensive metaphysical evaluation refers to all realities, it provides no grounds upon which to distinguish in favor of present action; the moral claim that potential future beauty should be sacrificed for the present cannot be justified. Thus, it may be said that the agent ought to maximize unity-in-diversity as such. But it may also be said that the agent ought to maximize the beauty of present activity. If present beauty could be sacrificed for the future, the best activity would not be maximal in beauty but maximal in the *pursuit of beauty*; similarly, the character of future activities to which one should seek to contribute would not be their maximal beauty but their maximal pursuit of beauty. The comprehensive evaluative variable would not be unity-in-diversity but the pursuit thereof. Every future event, when it arrives, is present, and if the best decision does not maximize present beauty, maximal beauty cannot be the good. But maximal beauty must be the good; otherwise there is no point in pursuing it. There can be, I conclude, no substantive difference between the choice which maximizes present beauty and the choice which pursues maximal beauty in reality as such. To seek maximal contribution to the future is to maximize the present instance, and the same categorically required choices may be identified in either way. Each actual occasion, says Whitehead, "is initiated by an enjoyment of the past as alive in itself and is terminated by an enjoyment of itself as alive in the future" (Whitehead 1961, 193).

I should be clear that this proposal fulfills the formal condition for an acceptable view of happiness that was specified at the conclusion of chapter 4, namely, that good for an individual should be morally defined and implied by a comprehensive principle for understanding and evaluating human activity. If unity-in-diversity is the comprehensive variable, so that maximal unity-in-diversity is the comprehensive evaluative principle, then good for an individual (or happiness) is in no way solely a matter of preference but can only be maximal unity-in-diversity realized within that individual's experience. It might be thought, then, that the argument has arrived at a coincidence of virtue and happiness. In the previous paragraph I said that activity which pursues maximal unity-in-diversity is maximally beautiful, and I have now said that maximal beauty in the agent is happiness. But note that happiness is the good for an individual, while the equation for which I have argued is between virtue and the maximal beauty of present activity. Happiness is appropriately defined, with Dewey, as "individuality-in-association," where this means the maximal unity-in-diversity over the course of a person's life. A swallow, as Aristotle taught us, does not make a summer. Also, the increase of unity-in-diversity experienced over the course of one's life might well be called, without violence to Dewey, "growth," so that happiness may be defined as maximal growth. A coincidence between virtue and happiness would obtain only if the activity which pursues maximal beauty for all subsequent realities is also the activity which pursues maximal beauty in just those subsequent activities which will be members of the acting individual, and nothing which has been said implies that *these* two purposes are coincident.

Still, the suggestion that virtue and happiness coincide has merit, because the coordinated life of an individual may, for the most part, be considered analogous to a concrete experience or activity. By virtue of its self-consciousness, each human action is implicitly or explicitly aware that its greatest effects upon the world will be within subsequent experiences of the individual of which it is a part. Therefore, each concrete human decision in association with the past and future implies a larger decision about the purpose of one's individual life in association with the wider world. Generally speaking, the life of an individual may be considered analogous to an aesthetic whole; it is continuously other-determined by its relations to the wider world and, through its larger purpose, makes a self-determined contribution beyond itself. This is simply an application to self-conscious existence of Whitehead's general claim that values are achieved by coordination into "societies of societies, and societies of societies of societies"—into enduring, complex associations. The individual is a temporally ordered or "personal" society.

To some, this conclusion will seem suspect, because it seems apparent that virtue sometimes requires a sacrifice of one's own happiness. There are, I think, circumstances in which this is true, especially those in which pursuit of beauty as such requires a sacrifice of the agent's life. The analogy between a concrete activity and a human's life is not complete, and for this reason one must use the qualifier "generally speaking" or "for the most part" when asserting a coincidence of virtue and happiness. Accordingly, one must be clear that the supreme ethical prescription cannot be stated "maximize one's own happiness," as indeed it may be stated "maximize the beauty of present action." The only equivalent to "maximize the beauty of present action" is "pursue maximal beauty in the future as such." But the analogy between individual and activity implies that the situations in which virtue and happiness do not coincide are more infrequent than is often thought. Virtue may indeed require the sacrifice of certain enjoyments that an individual wants, but these enjoyments may not constitute the individual's maximal unity-in-diversity. Thus, the apparent sacrifice of certain enjoyments is not, in a profound sense, sacrifice at all; it is only a sacrifice of the lesser for the greater self. Whitehead holds that one's commitment to the comprehensive metaphysical principle, the "telos of the universe," brings one's life into a fundamental harmony with "the way things are" and that this harmony means a profound strengthening of the individual's unity-in-diversity. Whitehead calls this profound happiness "peace," a "satisfaction deeper than joy or sorrow." "Peace is a quality of mind steady in its reliance that fine action is treasured in the nature of things" (Whitehead 1961, 172, 274).

Dewey is clear that the comprehensive moral principle requires pursuit of maximal individuality-in-association (maximal happiness) for all. This conclusion is one expression of Dewey's empirical pragmatism, because the latter entails that only human experience is valuable. In an appropriation of Dewey to an evaluative metaphysics, however, happiness becomes the peculiarly human form of a good whose realization in greater or lesser measure is coextensive with reality as such. Strictly speaking, the comprehensive moral imperative requires pursuit of maximal contingency-in-association, or beauty as such. As I will now try to show, however, there is merit in Dewey's suggestion that human activity ought to aim at maximal happiness for all, and this because aesthetic values are achieved through enduring complex associations. At least, Dewey's prescription follows if, with Whitehead, one holds that human action enjoys especially pronounced possibilities for value.

Whitehead distinguishes four grades of events or realities in the world, compared according to their exercise of freedom and, therefore, their possibilities for unity-in-diversity. In the lower two grades, inorganic and vegetable, these possibilities are severely limited. The dominating purpose of such events is the mere survival of the association (the stone, the tree) of which they are primarily a part. This is not to deny great natural beauty in the wilderness or the seashore. But a tree or a seashore is not a concrete event; the beauty found in the natural world is a composition realized in animal or human experience and is unknown to or unrealized in the constituent inorganic or vegetable events. Nonhuman animal experience enjoys greater freedom and, therefore, rises to greater unity-in-diversity. But self-conscious experience "immensely extends this concept," permitting purposes far transcending survival and, therefore, marked unity-in-diversity that results from pursuit of the better and the best. Individuality, in the sense of pronounced uniqueness, is a term applicable only to human events. "The distinction between men and animals is in one sense only a difference in degree. But the extent of the degree makes all the difference. The Rubicon has been crossed" (Whitehead 1938, 36, 38).

Given the crossing of the Rubicon, it follows from the aesthetic character of reality that the subhuman world achieves its greatest value when it is so ordered as to permit maximal human possibilities. The universe achieves its values by coordination into causal complexity. Thus, the comprehensive requirement to pursue maximal beauty may be translated into what I will call the *maximal happiness ideal*: human action ought to aim at maximal happiness for all (in the long run, by implication). With this translation, process metaphysics may appropriate Dewey's ethic.

It should be emphasized that the translation is effected solely for the purposes of ethical deliberation; it provides a basis upon which to decide which choices are categorically required. It does *not* imply that only human happiness is good. Precisely this implication is the aspect of Dewey's ethic which was denied in the move to a metaphysical evaluation. Indeed, only because all things are in some measure unities-in-diversity—and, therefore, in some measure good as such—can all things contribute to human happiness. By the same token, the destruction or sacrifice of potential subhuman value is morally justified *only* if this is required to maximize the happiness of all. The intrinsic goodness of all existence, in other words, proscribes such sacrifice when happiness can be maximized without it. Far from condoning every invasion of nature that is executed in the name of human purposes, the maximal happiness ideal permits such activity only when human potentialities, in the long run, are thereby greater than they could otherwise be.

In fact, maximal human happiness depends upon a considerable respect and appreciation for nature. Self-conscious freedom has permitted intentional exploitation of the earth in vast measure for the sake of human settlement. But the extent to which human existence depends upon a natural order of "societies, harmoniously requiring each other" (Whitehead 1978, 142) has recently become all the more apparent as the accumulated effects of industry, technology, and population growth have presented major "environmental" problems. Also, those who have the capacity to destroy vast natural aggregates simultaneously have the capacity to appreciate vast natural beauty. If a species of whales becomes extinct while whalers become prosperous, the potential loss to human happiness is great, and only if greater human possibilities are created can the deed be justified. Because of its abstract character, this discussion cannot settle any specific conflict between natural preservation and economic production. But much of the latter that pretends to be human progress may well be proscribed by the maximal happiness ideal.

It is also important to stress that this ideal is a justifiable guide to ethical deliberation only because human existence "crosses the Rubicon." If the difference between humans and some subhumans were slight (if, for instance, humans were only slightly superior to nonhuman primates), it would not be clear that the appearance of humans represents the maximal importance of subhuman existence as such. Indeed, the human species might then be the result of some more particular fortuitous coordination. In the absence of humans, for instance, it would not be true that subhuman existence should be so ordered as to maximize the enjoyment of primates, although it might be true that the ordering should be such as to maximize the enjoyment of animals. In short, extreme and enduring inequality of potential is the essential condition for assuming the aesthetic subordination of one kind of existence to another. For this reason, there is no general justification for aristocratic principles, for subordination of one group of humans to the happiness of another, whether the basis be that of birth, education, technological achievement, or some other. Granting that inequalities of potential exist among human individuals, these inequalities are too slight and too subject to change (they are neither extreme nor enduring) to conclude that the maximal happiness of one group is coincident with the maximal importance of the rest. Human inequality is due to circumstances more particular than aristocratic principles assume. With respect to the teleology of the universe, humans are in principle equals, and the proper guide for ethical deliberation is maximal happiness as such.

Given the extreme and enduring superiority of human activity and the aesthetic character of reality, it also follows that the comprehensive principle may be translated for deliberative purposes into pursuit of maximal human association, maximal beauty shared or communicated between or among human individuals. Since humans have the greatest potentialities for unity-in-diversity, human activities also add most to the possibilities of others. Indeed, were human existence isolated from the effects of the human community, the complexities of subhuman existence alone would permit human individuality only in some minimal measure. The higher possibilities of specifically human purpose emerge only by virtue of the complexity appropriated from previous human achievements. Nor is this conclusion altered by the fact that some individuals have greater innate capacities than others. Significant development of those capacities is possible only because other humans contribute to their exercise. The potential in Aristotle's mind was remarkable, but his achievements would not have been noteworthy in the absence of Plato and the academy. This is, then, simply a way to agree with Dewey's claim that intelligence or self-consciousness, the distinctively human characteristic, is itself a function of association. Since causal complexity is greater insofar as it increases human possibilities, it is also greater insofar as it includes human achievements.

I will call unity-in-diversity, insofar as it is shared among humans, "the public world," although in doing so I should stress that the term "public" takes on a different meaning than is found in Dewey's formulation. For Dewey the public consists of all those who are recipients of important indirect consequences of associated activity; shared worlds may be private insofar as the consequences are direct. I use the term "public" to designate the world created by *any* human communication or association, so that private worlds are those peculiar or limited to some one or another given human individual. The maximal happiness ideal, then, may be reformulated as the *maximal public ideal*, in accord with which activity seeks to maximize the public world (in the long run, by implication).

As with the maximal happiness ideal, this reformulation is effected solely for the purposes of moral deliberation. Just as the former does not imply that only happiness is good, so the maximal public ideal does not assert that happiness is constituted solely by human communication. On the contrary, private constituents of happiness have been implied. Included in these are the nonshared aspects of the individual's dialogue with himself or herself. If, as I have said, relations to self are far more complete than those to other humans, then each human individual is the only person who enjoys most of what he or she achieves. Moreover, some of the dialogue with self should *not* be humanly shared. The public world is better served if individuals have times of preparation for the public and a realm of privacy protected from the sight of other people. The maximal public ideal prescribes the pursuit of a private dialogue with oneself in whatever measure is required for maximizing the happiness created by human communication.

Also included in private happiness (at least on the whole) are the sustaining relations of human existence to the human body and, through it, to the rest of the subhuman world. The suffering that can be inflicted through disturbance within the human body indicates the extent to which general biological health and "material" security constitute happiness, although the fact that these ends dominate the lives of most people in the contemporary world indicates how far short of its possibilities the human race remains. The maximal public ideal prescribes due regard for the biological and "material" conditions of human existence, recognizing that these yield their own measure of self-enjoyment and are preconditions for substantial human sharing.

Subhuman existence not only sustains human life, it also enriches human happiness. Nature offers a world to be understood in human science, a world to be explored, cultivated, and appreciated for its own concrete forms of beauty. Consequently, the maximal public ideal requires the measure of attention to subhuman existence that is consistent with these contributions. In large measure, however, these relations are not private but properly a part of the public world; they yield happiness beyond some minimal degree because nature is, as it were, taken into the human community. The use of nature is enhanced by the community of craftsmen and technicians, the understanding of nature by the scientific community, the appreciation of nature by communication among poets and naturalists.

In any event, the reality of private happiness, either through relations to oneself or to subhuman existence, does not compromise the teleological priority of the public world. Teleologically speaking, private happiness should be pursued as a precondition for maximizing the public world, because in this way one is pursuing maximal happiness. Stated as a telos to be pursued, the maximal public ideal defines an associational order in which the happiness of all is maximized because each maximally inherits from and contributes to the individuality of others. "One general end," says Whitehead, "is that these variously coordinated groups should contribute to the complex pattern of community life, each in virtue of its own peculiarity. In this way, individuality gains the effectiveness which issues from coordination, and freedom obtains power necessary for its perfection." Whitehead calls this "the hope of statesmen, the solution which the long course of history is patiently disclosing" (Whitehead 1961, 67). The discussion has arrived at an appropriation of Dewey's ideal of democracy. Illustrated best for him by the scientific community at its best, this ideal also calls for associations that maximize the extent to which the individuality of each contributes to the individuality of all. Democracy will be tested, Dewey says, by two questions: "How numerous and varied are the interests that are consciously shared? How full and free is the interplay with other forms of association?" (Dewey 1944, 83). The same two questions would test conformity to the maximal public ideal.

As with Dewey's ideal, this one implies a political liberalism that is reformed rather than established in character. We have already seen that happiness or self-interest is in no respect solely a matter of preference but is defined by the criterion of maximal unity-in-diversity (or growth, or individuality-in-association) of the individual in question, so that putative self-interests may be distinguished from genuine ones insofar as they fail to maximize one's enjoyment of beauty. It is, of course, the maximal happiness of all in the genuine sense that is prescribed and reformulated as the ideal of the maximal public. As with Dewey, then, this ideal preserves the liberal values of freedom and individuality but reinterprets both. "The hope of statesmen," to repeat Whitehead's words, is one in which "individuality gains the effectiveness which issues from coordination, and freedom obtains power necessary for its perfection." This is not freedom as simply the absence of coercion by other humans; it is freedom as the opportunity for unity-in-diversity or, as Whitehead likes to say, "fine action" (see, e.g., Whitehead 1978, 274). It is not individuality as the pursuit of preferences. It is individuality as the achievement of unity-in-diversity effective for the future, as action that is fine because it pursues the maximal public world and thereby conforms to the teleology of the universe.

Political Theory

If it is true that a metaphysical formulation indebted to Whitehead and Hartshorne provides a justification for something very like Dewey's democratic ideal, it follows that this perspective also implies something very like his theory of associations, at least insofar as Dewey's theory is informed by the democratic ideal. His theory distinguishes between governmental (or second-order) and nongovernmental associations and, within the latter class, between consumption-regarding and community-regarding associations. Further, the democratic ideal implies that the telos of the social order is to maximize community-regarding associations. I will now try briefly to suggest that similar distinctions and a similar conclusion follow from the maximal public ideal.

Because pursuit of the maximal public world is a moral imperative, it does not necessarily define human activity. It is the character of self-conscious activity that it may misunderstand itself and, therefore, may choose alternatives that are categorically proscribed. Thus, some measure of coerceable order is morally prescribed. Since maximal unity-in-diversity is morally comprehensive, coerceable order is morally justified insofar as it is required by the maximal public world. In the larger community, this order is provided by the state, which we may define as that association whose identifying purpose consists in setting the coerceable conditions for all associations. Moreover, it may be argued that a larger community in which all individuals were always moral would still include such purposeful ordering (although coercion would, given such ideal circumstances, never be needed). The knowledge with which individuals act is incurably fragmentary. Notwithstanding even the best of intentions, none of the individuals within the community could know sufficiently the circumstances and probable consequences of his or her action so as to make those choices which, given sufficient knowledge, might maximize unity-in-diversity. The fragmentary character of human existence implies accidental evil, evil that is not moral evil because it is no one's moral fault. Also, as we noted during the discussion of Gewirth, the consequences of any given activity wait in significant measure upon other activities that are in principle unknowable, so that maximal good requires in significant measure agreements of convention (e.g., regarding traffic rules). For both of these reasons, a plurality of moral individuals would, in the absence of the state, fail to create a public world to the maximal possible extent. More precisely stated, the moral intentions of such individuals would imply purposeful ordering of associational life as such. Whether individuals are moral or not, an association to which all individuals must belong, the involuntary association of the state, is morally required.

The extent to which ordering by the state should occur is, with Dewey, historically contingent. Again with Dewey, if the contemporary situation includes associations of unprecedented scope and complexity, the matters to which the state should be attentive will also be unprecedented, because the extent of unknown and unknowable circumstances and consequences is vastly increased. Nonetheless, there is a prima facie case for voluntariness in associations, where "voluntariness" means the freedom to be or not to be a participant in the association in question. Maximizing the public world *is* the maximization of freedom. Consequently, freedom to choose the associations in which one is a member is prima facie important if one is to be maximally individual in one's particular circumstances for the sake of the public world. In saying this, one must also stress that freedom in association is not exhausted by voluntariness. Rather, freedom is opportunity for individuality and, therefore, involves the character of interaction within a given association as well as whether one chooses to participate. Thus, the state, although involuntary in membership, may be otherwise free in significant measure or respects. Insofar as its purpose is executed through discussion and debate in which the individuality of its members is cultivated, it creates the public world, and this is simply to affirm democratic government, in Dewey's sense. All other things being equal, however, voluntariness of association remains important, so that governmental activity is, in principle, teleologically subservient to voluntary associations which maximize the public world.

Theoretically significant distinctions within the class of nongovernmental associations must, of course, be derived from the maximal public ideal. This ideal prescribes maximal contribution to the world communicated among humans *in the long run*. The italicized implication is important because, in the short run, there are two, possibly competing, dimensions of this pursuit. There is, on the one hand, the content of what is communicated among human individuals and, on the other, how wide the sharing is. I will call these, respectively, the "character" and the "width" of the public world. On the one hand, the character may be greater or less, i.e., more or less beautiful. Other things being equal, character was greater when Shakespeare showed a sonnet to a friend than when virtually any others similarly share an effort at poetry. On the other hand, the communication may be more or less wide; it is wider when Shakespeare's sonnet is published than when it is shown to a friend. It should be emphasized that this distinction disappears in the long run and that character is the more inclusive term; greater width contributes to long-run character because it enhances the possibilities of more individuals to contribute to the public world. In the short run, however, there may be two alternative ways to maximize the long-run public world: increasing character at the expense of width, and increasing width at the expense of character. There may be situations in which width should be sacrificed for character, and vice versa. In some circumstances, attention to family or other intimate relationships should take precedence over participation in wider associations; in other circumstances, the imperative is reversed.

The distinction between short-run character and width implies a distinction within the possible purposes of nongovernmental associations. The public world pursued by an association may be more or less inclusive depending upon its width. A scholarly seminar in some more or less specialized subject pursues a relatively less inclusive public world; a public-interest association seeks to create a relatively more inclusive one. It might be objected that the seminar, through, say, the eventual publications of its members or through their work with students, intends to contribute to a wider public world than the seminar itself. But this contribution is not included within the distinguishing purpose of the association; it occurs through the participation of seminar members in other associations (e.g., universities or wider professional associations), so that the constitutive purpose of the seminar may be called less inclusive. On the other hand, should the seminar organize itself for the purpose of producing a volume of essays, the public world that it pursues becomes more inclusive.

I will call an association whose purpose is to maximize some public world a "public-regarding" association.[1] It might well be argued that the state falls within this class, because the democratic pursuit of a context for all associations seeks to maximize the widest possible public world. As we have seen, however, involuntary associations are limited in a sense that voluntary associations are not, so that state activity creates the widest public world only insofar as this is required to maximize voluntary creation of the public world. In order to preserve this distinction, I will reserve the term "public-regarding" for nongovernmental associations. I intend the term to be an alternative name for the class of associations which, in discussing Dewey's theory, I called "community-regarding." That class was said to consist in associations which pursue the content of human communication for its own sake, and this purpose *is* the intent to maximize some public world. Thus, the distinction between more or less inclusive public worlds implies a distinction within the class of public-regarding associations. In short-run terms, there is no moral ranking implied in the difference. As I have mentioned, there are circumstances which require a short-run sacrifice of width for character, and vice versa. Nonetheless, the distinction is theoretically significant, because width is important to long-run character. Less inclusive public-regarding associations are, in the long run, teleologically subservient to more inclusive ones.

All human associations create some public world in some measure, because there is no human association without human communication. But it does not follow that all nongovernmental associations are properly public-regarding. On the contrary, in some nongovernmental associations, communication is in part properly instrumental to diverse private worlds, is designed in significant measure to facilitate the independent relationships of individuals to themselves and to the subhuman world. I will call these associations "private-regarding," and I intend this to be an alternative name for the class of associations which, in discussing Dewey's theory, I called "consumption-regarding." The most prominent examples are what we commonly call economic or commercial institutions, although it should be repeated that private-regarding associations need not be profit-seeking. Even in the present social order, nonprofit health-delivery and charitable or social-service organizations are private-regarding. Moreover, if Dewey is correct that a dominantly corporate society may be democratic, in his sense, only if large com-

1. I owe this name and the implicit contrast with private-regarding associations to my colleague in the Social Ethics Seminar, George W. Pickering. For a published statement, see Pickering 1970. He is, of course, not responsible for the use which I make of his term.

mercial institutions are cooperatively or politically controlled or supervised, then to a large extent the class of private-regarding associations in such a society should be nonprofit.

It should be clear that the maximal public ideal does not disparage private-regarding associations. Maximal human sharing waits upon substantial unity-in-diversity within independent private worlds. Without biological health and a significant measure of material security, for instance, individuals enjoy only minimal release from attention to the necessities of survival. In addition, all human activities that are properly public-regarding (art, education, politics, religion) include certain relations to subhuman existence as a part of or condition for that activity (cathedrals or universities must be built), and the organizations which facilitate these relations might, at least in many cases, be properly private-regarding. But the maximal public ideal does imply that private-regarding associations should be teleologically subservient to public-regarding ones (consumption-regarding associations are teleologically subservient to community-regarding ones). Teleologically speaking, private worlds are preconditions for the maximal public world.

Assuming that the propriety of this set of distinctions would be confirmed by a more detailed discussion, we may say that the maximal public ideal informs a threefold division of the social order which is similar to that implied by Dewey's ideal of democracy. Government is distinguished as a second-order activity properly designed to order all associational life, and the significance of nongovernmental associations follows from the fact that voluntariness of association is an important aspect of freedom. Nongovernmental associations may be either public-regarding or private-regarding, depending upon whether their purpose is or is not solely to maximize some public world. Since all common American examples of commercial associations or their equivalents are private-regarding, it follows that "public-regarding" names a class of nongovernmental and noncommercial or independent associations. Since the comprehensive moral principle may be formulated as the maximal public ideal, it follows that involuntary associations and private-regarding associations are teleologically subservient to public-regarding ones. In short, independent associations are teleologically prior in the social order.

In addition, there is, within the class of independent associations, a relative distinction between the less inclusive and the more inclusive, such that the more inclusive are teleologically prior. In emphasizing this distinction, I do not mean to deny the different division of the independent sector, drawn during the discussion of Dewey's theory, into political-regarding associations and all others. Indeed, this latter distinction may be appropriated as a subdivision within the class of more inclusive, public-regarding associations. Political-regarding associations, then, are those which seek to maximize the public world created in the process of purposefully ordering associational life as such. Significant as this distinction is theoretically (because government is theoretically distinct) and urgent as it may be empirically (if, with Dewey, the maximal public ideal mandates significant reform or extension of the state's activity), it does not follow that political-regarding associations are teleologically prior. Although the widest possible public world is, in the long run, important to maximizing character, the widest possible public world is not maximized solely through the political process.

The appropriation of Dewey's theory of associations in accord with the maximal public ideal is schematically summarized in figure 5.

FIGURE 5
ASSOCIATIONS

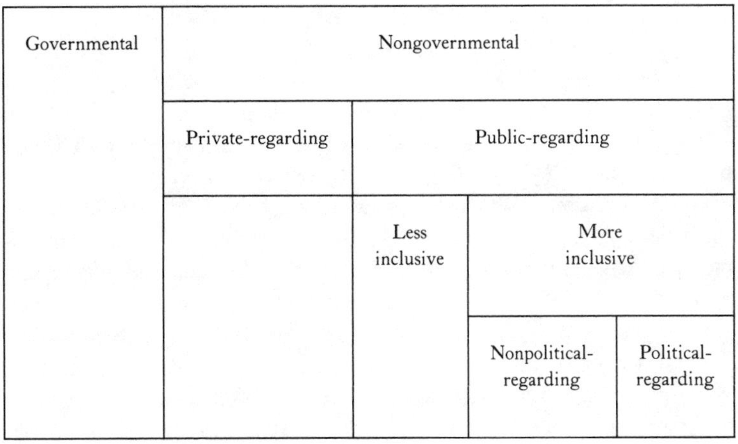

<table>
<tr><td rowspan="4">Governmental</td><td colspan="4">Nongovernmental</td></tr>
<tr><td rowspan="3">Private-regarding</td><td colspan="3">Public-regarding</td></tr>
<tr><td rowspan="2">Less inclusive</td><td colspan="2">More inclusive</td></tr>
<tr><td>Nonpolitical-regarding</td><td>Political-regarding</td></tr>
</table>

Finally, it is worth repeating that this fundamental threefold division of the social order contrasts sharply with the common trilogy of governmental, profit-seeking, and nonprofit institutions. The common set of distinctions appears to find its theoretical foundations in some version of established liberalism, either the nineteenth-century liberalism represented by the theory of Milton Friedman or an ambiguous mixture of this with the twentieth-century liberalism represented by the theory of Alan Gewirth. The pivotal difference represented by Dewey and the present appropriation of his theory is that independent associations now constitute the telos of associational life. The difference results from a turn to reformed liberalism in which human happiness is not solely a matter of preference but, to the contrary, is morally defined in accord with a comprehensive moral principle. As a consequence, the class of independent associations to be maximized is significantly more narrow than the commonly designated "third sector." Many of the latter, e.g., health-delivery and social-service organizations, are private-regarding. Public-regarding associations, in other words, are designed to develop, in Dewey's phrase, "the higher human capacities," those activities in which individuals may pursue the public world for its own sake and, thereby, maximize it.

Insofar as the discussion has successfully recommended this theory of associations, it has also recommended the importance of independent associations to political theory. For I have claimed that the social order should be so organized as to maximize just these associations. There is a certain injustice involved in calling this class the "third sector." At least in the sense that they are teleologically prior, public-regarding associations may properly be called the first sector of the human community.

Conclusion

At best, this chapter has done no more than suggest that Dewey's reformed liberalism may be given the metaphysical backing which, as I previously argued, is wanting in his own empirical pragmatism. I have sought with some care to show that a comprehensive moral principle must be a specification of a comprehensive evaluative variable that is metaphysical, but the character of this variable and the consequent moral and associational theory have been presented only in outline. Thus, the promise of a process metaphysics and of Dewey's political distinctions has been at best recommended. The fulfillment of that promise waits upon a more or less complete treatment of metaphysics, morality, and political theory.

Three of the matters which such a treatment must address are sufficiently central that they merit mention here. The first involves the concept of the public world. In the review of Dewey's theory, I noted that he does not explicitly discuss the move from a diversity of publics, one of which is created whenever associated activity has important indirect consequences, to *the* public, which is organized to order or supervise all associational life. In somewhat analogous fashion, this chapter has not discussed the relation between the diversity of public worlds, one of which is created whenever humans communicate, and *the* public world which is to be maximized. I have implied that *the* public world is, or may be treated as, a unity-in-diversity of which the diverse public worlds created are constituent parts. If this is the case, the public world is or implies a unity-in-diversity of immense complexity, and one might object that the fragmentariness of human understanding precludes the kind of calculation that would be required to pursue the maximization of such complexity. But human activity is inescapably particular and a comprehensive moral principle is inescapably general. In the nature of the case, then, judgment that is informed by but limited to the best that we can know is always involved in moral choice. Of course, it must be shown that the comprehensive principle is not so generally formulated that it is vacuous in practical deliberation. The attempt here to outline a theory of associations informed by the maximal public ideal is meant to provide at least initial evidence that the comprehensive principle recommended does indeed provide guidance to human choice. Beyond this, the practical import of the principle waits upon the formulation of more specific moral standards. Such standards are the focus of the third central matter I wish to mention and to which I will presently turn.

In the meantime, a philosophical question with respect to the public world as such remains: In what sense does this term refer to or imply a unity-in-diversity of which diverse human communications are constituent parts? Without an answer to this question, the comprehensive moral principle that has been asserted here is incoherent. Since the ideal of the maximal public is a reformulation of the imperative to maximize unity-in-diversity, the question, more precisely stated, is whether the diverse unities-in-diversity or activities of the world are constituent parts of any comprehensive unity-in-diversity. This issue returns the discussion to the religious character of the comprehensive metaphysical variable. It is because the variable in terms of which all possible existents are understood and evaluated requires a comprehensive or supreme instance that both Whitehead and Hartshorne are theists. The public world becomes a meaningful concept because diverse human communications are all a part of the divine unity-in-diversity. If a more or less complete metaphysical discussion could give good reason for that affirmation, it might then be said that the maximal public ideal finds its justification in the character of God. The definition of the term "God," a defense of its coherence, and an argument for the divine necessity are issues to which that more complete discussion must attend.

The second matter of central importance involves the charge of paternalism which the theory recommended here may anticipate from the advocates of established liberalism. At stake is the affirmation of freedom as fundamental to any adequate liberal theory. When the social order pursues a substantive telos, this objection runs, a collective decision regarding the good for all is in some sense implied. The freedom of those in the social order who do not affirm this telos is then compromised; their happiness is in some sense decided for them. Thus, genuine freedom is maximized only if the social order as such pursues no substantive ideal. It follows that associations should be designed simply to facilitate maximal opportunity for each individual to pursue happiness as he or she defines it.

But whether a social order is "paternalistic" depends entirely upon what understanding of freedom is presupposed in making the judgment. Only if one presumes, with established liberalism, that freedom is the opportunity to pursue solely preferential purposes does a substantive telos necessarily merit the indictment. If, to the contrary, freedom is positively correlated with the public world to which one is related (or, with Dewey, individuality is positively correlated with association), then the maximal public world is the only associational ideal in accord with which "individuality gains the effectiveness which issues from coordination and freedom obtains power necessary for its perfection" (Whitehead 1961, 67). With the political theory recommended here, the charge of paternalism might be turned back upon those who first advanced it. This reversal depends upon the assertion, with Dewey, that established liberalism is committed to the notion of the "separate individual." There is, I think, a relevant sense in which this assertion may be defended, although here I will attempt only to suggest the argument involved and why it implies that established liberalism must answer to one of its own favorite critiques.

In the theory recommended here, the supreme or comprehensive moral principle is also a comprehensive variable in accord with which human activity and association are understood. Because established liberalism affirms the preferential view of self-interest, its supreme moral principle is defined in terms of generic opportunity. It follows that human associations can be understood only in these generic terms, and human association (or relation to the public world) cannot be one of the solely preferential purposes for which generic capacities might be exercised. Association as such provides preconditions for preferential happiness. The established liberal view of happiness implies that self-interests are private, and it is in this sense that the individual is "separate." It also follows that these private interests cannot themselves be understood, and one might well argue that the notion of "preconditions" for such interests therefore makes no sense. But that is simply another way of saying that partialism is self-contradictory and, therefore, fallacious. If we are to speak at all of established liberalism as a theory which informs the social order, the appropriate conclusion is that self-interests are private. We may also conclude that such a social order is one in which private-regarding associations are teleologically prior.

But now assume that freedom is, in truth, positively correlated with the public world to which one is related. It follows that the established liberal order limits the range of human freedom, because it compromises the maximal public world. Established liberalism implies a collective decision in some sense which limits the range of purposes which individuals might pursue, and it is this limitation upon the good for all that might be called "paternalism." Clearly, this charge begs for more thorough discussion. More importantly, the reformed liberal understanding recommended here requires thorough development, especially with respect to prescriptions for the associational order, if its fundamental affirmation of human freedom is to be fully persuasive.

We come to the third matter of central importance to a more or less complete treatment: the formulation of moral and political standards of lesser generality than the comprehensive moral principle. Because human activity is incurably particular, a complete moral and political theory requires the specification of the comprehensive principle in ways that facilitate moral and political choice. Most fully pursued, specification to particular choices involves a contemporary practical science which takes the inquiry beyond theoretical questions into empirical analysis of specific contemporary conditions of human activity. Indeed, strictly speaking, any specification of metaphysical principles involves empirical premises. But if moral and political theory includes all claims that are implied in the character of human activity as such, an empirical premise (the character of human activity as such) has already been introduced in such theory. It is, incidentally, this empirical premise (that human existence, in comparison with subhuman existence, enjoys extreme and enduring superiority of potential) which informed my translation of the comprehensive moral principle into the maximal happiness and maximal public ideals. In somewhat similar fashion, a more complete theory must seek further specific standards, even if these are prima-facie in character, for moral and political choice.

Such a development of the maximal public ideal will also serve as a check upon the philosophical argument that has been presented. Should the consequence be standards for practical deliberation which are substantially at odds with widely accepted moral wisdom, and which are, in that sense, "counterintuitive," there will be reason to reexamine the reasoning through which the comprehensive moral principle has been formulated. Especially important in this regard will be the implied standards with respect to the distribution of opportunity for happiness. Moral theory which is teleological in character, which defines categorically required activity by the maximization of some comprehensive variable, is frequently criticized as counterintuitive with respect to questions of distributive justice. Ideally, or in the long run, the maximal public principle implies equal opportunity for happiness; it prescribes a social order in which the happiness of all is maximized because each maximally inherits from and maximally contributes to the individuality of all others. This ideal implies a prima-facie standard of equal opportunity in the short run. But the meaning of "equal opportunity" and the conditions under which exceptions to this prima-facie standard are permitted must be clarified before it can be determined whether the standard accords with widely accepted moral wisdom. Those issues illustrate the kind of question involved in the third central matter to which a more complete treatment of the reformed liberalism recommended here must attend.

Finally, the end of political theory is to inform associational activity, so that theory itself includes the imperative to develop a contemporary practical science. Although that pursuit lies beyond the scope of this work, practical implications of the maximal public ideal have already been suggested in saying that the common understandings of independent institutions appear to be informed by established rather than reformed theories of political liberalism. Insofar as those common understandings are effective in political life, the theory outlined here recommends changes in the social order. This is all the more the case if, as I am inclined to believe, common understandings of the third sector reflect the more or less pervasive effectiveness of established liberalism throughout the American social order, so that Dewey's general empirical judgment remains substantially correct: private-regarding associations dominate our contemporary life. If that is so, the theory recommended here provides the terms within which a more or less thorough critique of American associational life and its informing ideals might be advanced, thereby enhancing the possibility that the maximal public ideal might be more effectively entertained. In addition, the conviction will be expressed that public-regarding associations are, to appropriate the words of Tocqueville, not only "as necessary to the American people" as all others but also "more so."

Works Cited

Adams, E. M.
1980 "Gewirth on Reason and Morality." *Review of Metaphysics* 33:579–92.

Adams, James Luther
1971 "The Voluntary Principle in the Forming of American Religion." In Elwyn A. Smith, ed. *The Religion of the Republic*. Philadelphia: Fortress Press.

Barry, Brian
1965 *Political Argument*. London: Routledge and Kegan Paul.

Cobb, John B., Jr.
1982 *Process Theology as Political Theology*. Philadelphia: The Westminster Press.

Cobb, John B., Jr., and Schroeder, W. Widick
1981 *Process Philosophy and Social Thought*. Chicago: Center for the Scientific Study of Religion.

Commission on Private Philanthropy and Public Needs
1975 *Giving in America*. Report of the Commission on Private Philanthropy and Public Needs. Department of the Treasury.
1977 *Research Papers*. 5 volumes. Department of the Treasury.

Dewey, John
1930 *Human Nature and Conduct*. New York: Random House. Original publication: 1922.

1934 *Our Common Faith*. New Haven: Yale University Press.

1939 *Theory of Valuation*. Chicago: University of Chicago Press.

1944 *Democracy and Education*. New York: The Free Press.

1951 "Creative Democracy—The Task Before Us." Max H. Fisch, ed. *Classic American Philosophies*. New York: Appleton-Century-Crofts, 389–94.

1954 *The Public and Its Problems*. Chicago: Swallow Press. Original publication: 1927.

1957 *Reconstruction in Philosophy*. Boston: Beacon Press. Original publication: 1920.

1958 *Experience and Nature*. New York: Dover Publications. Original publication: 1929.

1962 *Individualism Old and New*. New York: Capricorn Books. Original publication: 1929.

1963a *Liberalism and Social Action*. New York: Capricorn Books. Original publication: 1935.

1963b *Experience and Education*. New York: Collier Books. Original publication: 1938.

Easton, David

1953 *The Political System*. New York: Alfred A. Knopf.

1965 *A Framework for Political Analysis*. Englewood Cliffs, N.J.: Prentice-Hall.

Frankena, William K.

1973 *Ethics*. Englewood Cliffs, N.J.: Prentice-Hall.

Friedman, Milton

1962 *Capitalism and Freedom*. Chicago: The University of Chicago Press.

Friedman, Milton, and Friedman, Rose

1981 *Free to Choose*. New York: Harcourt Brace Jovanovich.

Galbraith, John Kenneth

1973 *Economics and the Public Purpose*. Boston: Houghton Mifflin.

Gamwell, Franklin I.

1978 "Ethics, Metaphysics, and the Naturalistic Fallacy." In W. Widick Schroeder and Gibson Winter, eds. *Belief and Ethics*. Chicago: Center for the Scientific Study of Religion.

Geertz, Clifford

1973 *The Interpretation of Cultures*. New York: Basic Books.

Gewirth, Alan

1978 *Reason and Morality*. Chicago: University of Chicago Press.

Greenstone, J. David

1982 "The Transient and Permanent in American Politics: Standards, Interests, and the Concept of 'Public'." In J. David Greenstone, ed. *Public Values and Private Power in American Politics*. Chicago: University of Chicago Press, 3–33.

Hall, David

1973 *The Civilization of Experience*. New York: Fordham University Press.

Hare, R. M.

1961 *The Language of Morality*, revised edition. New York: Oxford University Press. Original publication: 1952.

1965 *Freedom and Reason*. New York: Oxford University Press.

Hartshorne, Charles

1937 *Beyond Humanism*. Lincoln: University of Nebraska Press.

1948 *The Divine Relativity*. New Haven: Yale University Press.

1962 *The Logic of Perfection*. LaSalle, Ill.: Open Court.

1970 *Creative Synthesis and Philosophic Method*. LaSalle, Ill.: Open Court.

Hartz, Louis

1955 *The Liberal Tradition in America*. New York: Harcourt Brace and World.

Horowitz, Robert
1963 "John Dewey." Leo Strauss and Joseph Cropsey, eds. *History of Political Philosophy*. Chicago: Rand McNally, 746–62.

Kariel, Henry S.
1977 *Beyond Liberalism. Where Relations Grow*. New York: Harper and Row.

Lindblom, Charles E.
1977 *Politics and Markets*. New York: Basic Books.

Lowi, Theodore J.
1969 *The End of Liberalism*. New York: W. W. Norton and Company.

MacIntyre, Alasdair
1981 *After Virtue*. Notre Dame, Ind.: University of Notre Dame Press.

Moore, G. E.
1968 *Principia Ethica*. Cambridge: Cambridge University Press. Original publication: 1903.

Nielsen, Waldemar A.
1979 *The Endangered Sector*. New York: Columbia University Press.

Ogden, Schubert M.
1971 "The Task of Philosophical Theology." In *The Future of Philosophical Theology*. Robert H. Evans, ed. Philadelphia: The Westminster Press, 55–84.
1979 *Faith and Freedom: Toward a Theology of Liberation*. Nashville: Abingdon.

Pickering, George W.
1970 "Voluntarism and the American Way." Occasional Paper No. 7. Washington, D.C.: Center for a Voluntary Society.

Robertson, D. B., ed.
1966 *Voluntary Associations: A Study of Groups in Free Societies*. Richmond, Va.: John Knox Press.

Schneewind, J. B.
1970 "Moral Knowledge and Moral Principles." *Knowledge and Necessity*. London: Macmillan.

Schroeder, W. Widick
1970 *Cognitive Structures and Religious Research.* East Lansing: Michigan State University Press.

Simon, John G., and Hansmann, Henry
1978 "The Role of the Non-Profit Corporation." *Yale Alumni Magazine and Journal.* April.

Smith, Constance, and Freedman, Anne
1972 *Voluntary Associations: Perspectives on the Literature.* Cambridge, Mass.: Harvard University Press.

Smith, John E.
1963 *The Spirit of American Philosophy.* New York: Oxford University Press.

Tocqueville, Alexis de
1945 *Democracy in America.* Vol. 2. New York: Alfred A. Knopf.

Unger, Roberto Mangabeira
1975 *Knowledge and Politics.* New York: The Free Press.

Veatch, Henry B.
1979 Book Review. *Ethics* 89:401–14.

Whitehead, Alfred North
1925 *Science and the Modern World.* New York: Macmillan.

1938 *Modes of Thought.* New York: Macmillan.

1961 *Adventures of Ideas.* New York: The Free Press. Original publication: 1933.

1978 *Process and Reality*, corrected edition, ed. David Ray Griffin and Donald Sherburne. New York: The Free Press. Original publication: 1929.

Wolff, Robert Paul
1968 *The Poverty of Liberalism.* Boston: Beacon Press.

Wolin, Sheldin S.
1968 *Politics and Vision.* Boston: Little, Brown.

Index